INTRODUCING
ISSUES WITH
OPPOSING
VIEWPOINTS®

# Christianity

Other books in the Introducing Issues
with Opposing Viewpoints series:

INTRODUCING
ISSUES WITH
OPPOSING
VIEWPOINTS®

# Christianity

Mike Wilson, *Book Editor*

Christine Nasso, *Publisher*
Elizabeth Des Chenes, *Managing Editor*

**GREENHAVEN PRESS**

*An imprint of Thomson Gale, a part of The Thomson Corporation*

THOMSON
™
GALE

Detroit • New York • San Francisco • New Haven, Conn. • Waterville, Maine • London

© 2008 The Gale Group.

*For more information, contact*
Greenhaven Press
27500 Drake Rd.
Farmington Hills, MI 48331-3535
Or you can visit our Internet site at http://www.gale.com

LIBRARY OF CONGRESS CATALOGING-IN-PUBLICATION DATA

Christianity / Mike Wilson, book editor.
    p. cm. — (Introducing issues with opposing viewpoints)
  Includes bibliographical references and index.
  ISBN-13: 978-0-7377-3874-2 (hardcover)
  1. Christianity.    I. Wilson, Mike, 1954-
  BR121.3.C47 2007
  270.8'3—dc22
                                                              2007036332

ISBN-10: 0-7377-3874-X (hardcover)

Printed in the United States of America

# Contents

# Chapter 3. What Is the Future of Christianity?

# Foreword

Indulging in a wide spectrum of ideas, beliefs, and perspectives is a critical cornerstone of democracy. After all, it is often debates over differences of opinion, such as whether to legalize abortion, how to treat prisoners, or when to enact the death penalty that shape our society and drive it forward. Such diversity of thought is frequently regarded as the hallmark of a healthy and civilized culture. As the Reverend Clifford Schutjer of the First Congregational Church in Mansfield, Ohio, declared in a 2001 sermon, "Surrounding oneself with only like-minded people, restricting what we listen to or read only to what we find agreeable is irresponsible. Refusing to entertain doubts once we make up our minds is a subtle but deadly form of arrogance." With this advice in mind, Introducing Issues with Opposing Viewpoints books aim to open readers' minds to the critically divergent views that comprise our world's most important debates.

Introducing Issues with Opposing Viewpoints simplifies for students the enormous and often overwhelming mass of material now available via print and electronic media. Collected in every volume is an array of opinions that capture the essence of a particular controversy or topic. Introducing Issues with Opposing Viewpoints books embody the spirit of nineteenth-century journalist Charles A. Dana's axiom: "Fight for your opinions, but do not believe that they contain the whole truth, or the only truth." Absorbing such contrasting opinions teaches students to analyze the strength of an argument and compare it to its opposition. From this process readers can inform and strengthen their own opinions, or be exposed to new information that will change their minds. Introducing Issues with Opposing Viewpoints is a mosaic of different voices. The authors are statesmen, pundits, academics, journalists, corporations, and ordinary people who have felt compelled to share their experiences and ideas in a public forum. Their words have been collected from newspapers, journals, books, speeches, interviews, and the Internet, the fastest growing body of opinionated material in the world.

Introducing Issues with Opposing Viewpoints shares many of the well-known features of its critically acclaimed parent series, Opposing Viewpoints. The articles are presented in a pro/con format, allowing readers to absorb divergent perspectives side by side. Active reading questions preface each viewpoint, requiring the student to approach the material thoughtfully and carefully. Useful charts, graphs, and cartoons supplement each article. A thorough introduction provides readers with crucial background on an issue. An annotated bibliography points the reader toward articles, books, and Web sites that contain additional information on the topic. An appendix of organizations to contact contains a wide variety of charities, nonprofit organizations, political groups, and private enterprises that each hold a position on the issue at hand. Finally, a comprehensive index allows readers to locate content quickly and efficiently.

Introducing Issues with Opposing Viewpoints is also significantly different from Opposing Viewpoints. As the series title implies, its presentation will help introduce students to the concept of opposing viewpoints, and learn to use this material to aid in critical writing and debate. The series' four-color, accessible format makes the books attractive and inviting to readers of all levels. In addition, each viewpoint has been carefully edited to maximize a reader's understanding of the content. Short but thorough viewpoints capture the essence of an argument. A substantial, thought-provoking essay question placed at the end of each viewpoint asks the student to further investigate the issues raised in the viewpoint, compare and contrast two authors' arguments, or consider how one might go about forming an opinion on the topic at hand. Each viewpoint contains sidebars that include at-a-glance information and handy statistics. A Facts About section located in the back of the book further supplies students with relevant facts and figures.

Following in the tradition of the Opposing Viewpoints series, Greenhaven Press continues to provide readers with invaluable exposure to the controversial issues that shape our world. As John Stuart Mill once wrote: "The only way in which a human being can make some approach to knowing the whole of a subject is by hearing what can be said about it by persons of every variety of opinion and studying all modes in which it can be looked at by every character of mind. No wise man ever acquired his wisdom in any mode but this." It is to this principle that Introducing Issues with Opposing Viewpoints books are dedicated.

# Introduction

*"Doctrinal differences have broken friendships, destroyed families, divided churches even brought nations to war. . . . [However] the church neither can be unified nor can it witness effectively to the world without a common doctrine. Doctrine is another name for reality and churches will stay together and act effectively only if they live according to right doctrine. . . . If Christians are to be one body in any meaningful sense and if they are to get anything useful done, they have to be dogmatic. To stop worrying about right doctrine is a luxury the church cannot afford."*

—David Mills, editor of *Touchstone: A Magazine of Mere Christianity*

Whether one is a conservative, moderate, or liberal Christian or not a Christian at all, the quote above illustrates a fundamental question that looms in the background of most of the opposing viewpoints in *Introducing Issues with Opposing Viewpoints: Christianity*. It is, What is true Christian doctrine?

Many of the authors of the opposing viewpoints in this volume claim to base their views on an interpretation of Christian doctrine. But when opposing interpretations are reached from the same sources, how does one discern who is right and who is wrong?

## The Bible

One source of authority relied upon by all Christians is the Bible. It has been estimated that Americans purchased about 25 million Bibles during 2005. Author Philip Jenkins points out in *The New Faces of Christianity: Believing the Bible in the Global South* that divisions in Christianity often are based upon different views of authority and the position of the Bible as authority. According to a 2006 survey of Americans by Barna Research, 74 percent of women and 62 percent of men believe the Bible is completely accurate in all of its teachings.

Belief in the Bible does not result in uniform points of view, however. According to World Christian Database Center for the Study of Global Christianity, there are 635 different Christian sects in the United States alone, and there are over fifty different translations of the Bible. Protestant Bibles contain thirty-nine books in the Old Testament and Catholic Bibles contain forty-six Old Testament books. Catholics also place importance on traditions and the teaching authority of the Church that Protestants do not. In articles appearing in this collection, authors with opposing opinions often cite the Bible in support of their views, but produce different interpretations.

Another aspect of defining Christian doctrine for those relying upon the Bible as authority is the method used to understand the Bible. Some believe that the Bible should be interpreted literally while others conclude that some biblical stories are merely allegories, parables, or metaphors. According to a 2006 Gallup poll, 49 percent of Americans believe the Bible is the inspired word of God, 28 percent believe the Bible is literally true, and 19 percent believe the Bible is an "ancient book of fables." Whether one interprets the Bible literally is important when deciding whether Christianity should change when society changes.

## Customs or Timeless Truths?

Society's ideas about proper behavior have changed from time to time in the course of history. Are some church teachings and admonitions in the Bible just a reflection of what was customary at the time rather than timeless truths? For example, I Corinthians asserts that women should cover their hair in church. Is this custom essential to Christian doctrine or only what was proper at the time? During the times described in both the Old Testament and the New Testament, slavery was an accepted practice. Therefore, can one interpret slavery as Christian? How does one sort out the timeless truths from codes of behavior that are merely customary at a certain time and place?

The role of women in society also has changed since the Bible was written. Today, gender equality is the norm, but for many centuries, men dominated public life, including church governance, and women played subordinate roles and could not be priests. Is the prohibition against ordaining women essential to Christianity or merely a custom of the past?

Society's acceptance of sexuality in the twenty-first century also may conflict with traditional Christian teachings. According to Barna

Research, 59 percent of Americans surveyed thought enjoying sexual thoughts and fantasies was morally acceptable. The National Center for Health Statistics found that only 4 percent of Americans aged twenty to fifty-nine have never had sex and only 11 percent of never-married adults remain chaste. However, the Catholic Church requires priests to be both unmarried and celibate—according to the survey, a practice that only a small percentage of their parishioners adhere to. Is priestly celibacy just a custom or essential to Christian doctrine?

Society's view of homosexuality also has changed. In the past Western society generally disapproved of same-sex relationships, and Christianity treated such relationships as a sin. However, a 2007 Gallup poll found that 59 percent of Americans thought homosexual relations should be legal, 57 percent thought homosexuality was an acceptable lifestyle, 47 percent thought homosexual relations were morally acceptable, and 46 percent thought gay marriage should be as valid, and have the same legal rights, as traditional marriage between heterosexual couples. Is heterosexual marriage essential to Christian doctrine?

Jenkins notes that "Christian denominations worldwide have been deeply divided over issues of gender, sexual morality, and homo-sexuality. These debates illustrate a sharp global division, with many North American and European churches willing to accommodate liberalizing trends in the wider society, while their African and Asian counterparts prove much more conservative."

## Christianity's Role in Democracy

Another area of conflict in Christianity is the role religion should play in democracy. In a democratic government, public laws that regulate behavior are adopted by a majority vote. Christian doctrine also has rules that regulate behavior. Are Christians obligated to guarantee that public laws reflect Christian doctrine?

Americans have freedom to choose religions other than Christianity, or no religion at all. In America, there are estimated to be 6 to 7 million Muslims, 5 to 6 million Jews, and 2 to 3 million Buddhists. If religion mixes with politics, some argue, those who govern will be able to force upon others the religious views they hold, undermining nonbelievers' freedoms. In fact, many of the European colonists who settled North America came here because governments in Europe favored certain religions and persecuted others. The U.S. Constitution prohibits religious tests as a qualification for those attaining public office and prohibits Congress from making or recognizing laws that establish a state religion. Thomas Jefferson, one of the Founding Fathers, famously put forth that there should be "a great wall of separation between church and state."

At the same time, many Christians believe that morality is based upon religion, and therefore in order to be moral, government should reflect the values of Christian doctrine. Can't Christianity, they might ask, serve as well or better as a guide for structuring society than, say, philosophy, political theory, or sociology? Some Christians believe that a proper understanding of Christianity obligates them to engage in political activism. Some believe that Christians should only vote for other Christians with doctrinal views like their own. Other Christians go even further, claiming that Christianity is God's law and therefore the United States should be a theocracy instead of a democracy.

Because there are different ideas about Christian doctrine, however, politically active Christians may have opposite views about the same social and political issues. As you read this collection of essays, note how authors often rely upon the same sources—Christian doctrine, the Bible, the Constitution—to defend opposing viewpoints.

# Chapter 1

# What Is the Role of Christianity in the World?

*Cardinal John J. O'Connor of New York shows compassion and concern at the site of the devastated fuel depot at Dora in Christian east Beirut in 1989.*

# Christians Should Be Politically Active

Alan Johnson and
Catherine Candisky

*"God has a plan. If I vote in line with his will . . . he's going to win."*

In the following viewpoint, Alan Johnson and Catherine Candisky, citing results from a poll conducted by the *Columbus Dispatch* in 2006, explain why conservative Christians feel compelled to be politically active. Ohio Christians quoted by the authors explain that what they consider to be wrong decisions on issues such as same-sex marriage, abortion, and public display of the Ten Commandments threaten Christian values. These Christians consider it a religious duty to support candidates who reflect their values. The authors are reporters for the *Columbus Dispatch*.

**AS YOU READ, CONSIDER THE FOLLOWING QUESTIONS:**
1. According to the Christian radio host quoted by the authors, what issue created the "tipping point" propelling Christians to become politically active?
2. To which political party do most conservative Christians belong, according to the author?

Like many conservative Christians, Marilyn Reinking grew increasingly uncomfortable with some of what she saw in American society. Abortion. Same-sex marriage. Pornography. The Ten Commandments removed from public places. Prayer banned in public schools. To Reinking, the values she held most dear were under attack. So the 70-year-old retired nurse from Fairfield [Ohio] did something: She got involved in politics, through the Internet, in her Butler County community, in her church. "I really think that it's being aware that our freedoms are being eroded," she said. "The freedom for Christians is being attacked, and that concerns me. I believe our country was based on the Bible.

## Pushed to the Edge

Conservative Christians, the vast majority of whom are Republicans, offer multiple reasons for how they coalesced into a political powerhouse in Ohio and nationally during recent years. The movement has charismatic and influential leaders, but average Ohioans are the ground troops in this spiritual battle with earthly weapons. Many politically active Christians who, like Reinking, took part in a Dispatch Poll said they felt pushed to the edge by events unfolding in society, government, the courts and the entertainment world. Two out of three who responded to the mail survey said they feel it's important that Ohio's governor have strong religious beliefs. More than 60 percent said their religious beliefs are important in deciding how to vote, and 26 percent said their level of political activity increased in the past five years.

## Erosion of Values

Like many, 50-year-old Dave Clary, of the Cleveland suburb of Strongsville, said he's pushing back against the erosion of his values. "I've become more active in my church. I've become more involved in my neighborhood. I talk to my friends," said the father of three. Conservative Christians sat on the political sidelines for decades, but that's changed in recent years, Clary said. "The Christian majority is sick and tired of things like same-sex marriage and the (removal of

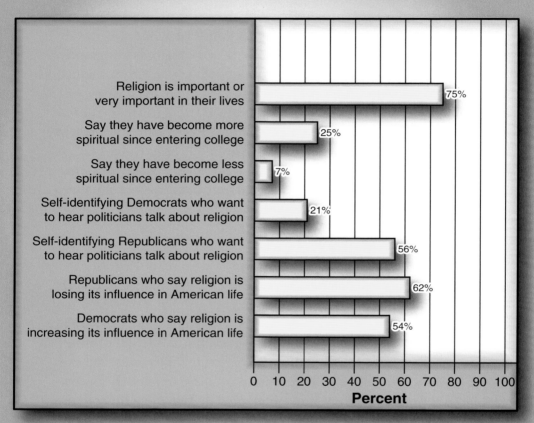

## Survey of College Students on Religion and Politics

*A majority of college students surveyed, both Democrats and Republicans, are concerned about the moral direction of the United States.*

| | Percent |
|---|---|
| Religion is important or very important in their lives | 75% |
| Say they have become more spiritual since entering college | 25% |
| Say they have become less spiritual since entering college | 7% |
| Self-identifying Democrats who want to hear politicians talk about religion | 21% |
| Self-identifying Republicans who want to hear politicians talk about religion | 56% |
| Republicans who say religion is losing its influence in American life | 62% |
| Democrats who say religion is increasing its influence in American life | 54% |

Taken from: 2006 poll, Harvard University Institute of Politics

the) Ten Commandments in the courthouse," he said. "Two people get upset, and the ACLU [American Civil Liberties Union] comes in. People are tired of things like one guy with a lawyer changing the entire face of a government building because of the Ten Commandments. What the hell was it hurting?"

## Clash of Worldviews
Bob Burney, who hosts a Christian radio call-in program on WRFD

(880 AM) in Columbus, hears the complaint a lot. "It's the clash of two worldviews," he said. "Things have been declared to be unconstitutional that have been constitutional for 200 years," he said. "Evangelical Christians are energized by their very strong perception that those on the left want to remove the Godly heritage that we have and move to a completely secular state." The tipping point for many was a

2003 Massachusetts court decision allowing gay couples to marry. "Christians consider the institute of marriage to be sacred, and if the courts can come in and tamper with it, what else might they do?" asked Tom Minnery, senior vice president of public policy for Focus on the Family. The conservative evangelical group is conducting a voter-registration drive in Ohio and seven other battleground states this fall. "We can't push back by being silent," he said. But Burney said voter enthusiasm among conservative Christians seems less intense this year. "I don't see the energy I saw in the last presidential election," he said.

## Candidates Should Have Christian Values

Poll respondent Heather Tester, a 31-year-old special education teacher and mother of three from Wauseon in northwestern Ohio, said her religious beliefs fueled her interest in politics. She said she votes for candidates who share her views, particularly her opposition to same-sex marriage and abortion rights and her support for the Iraq war. She said she is backing Republican J. Kenneth Blackwell for governor because "he backs everything I believe in." Phil Burress, head of Cincinnati-based Citizens for Community Values, said conservative Christians tend to side with the GOP [Grand Old Party, a nickname for the Republican Party], but the party should not take that for granted.

"If the Republican Party thinks that people of faith belong to them, they got another [thing] . . . coming." He said if the GOP doesn't "find its rudder in the next two years, it's going to drift for many years to come." While Burress's followers don't have a rallying call like same-sex marriage this year, as they did in 2004 when Ohioans voted to ban the practice, he predicted they will remain engaged.

## Call to Arms

"This is a call to arms," he said. "The involvement of the faith community is on the rise." The call is going out more often these days as conservative clergy members and lay supporters hold revival-style meetings with political overtones and rally the faithful through exten-

*Many Christians become politically active by protesting actions they consider immoral.*

sive Internet networks, phone banks and thousands of flyers inserted in church bulletins. At a recent rally at the Columbus Christian Center on the Northeast Side, black and white pastors from across the nation implored followers to keep the faith and keep up the political pressure that helped elect President [George W.] Bush and pass marriage amendments in numerous states. "You can't stop. You can't slow down," Pastor Derek McCoy, of High Impact Leadership in Maryland, urged the faithful. "The alarm has to keep sounding, folks." In the audience was Ryan Hicks of Grove City, who was 17 when he volunteered to work for the Bush and marriage amendment campaigns in 2004. Hicks was so energized by the political process that in the May primary he ran for and was elected to the Franklin County GOP Central Committee, "I don't want to shy away from politics. Christians have shied away from politics and look what happened." Hicks works as a pastoral assistant at Potter's House church on the West Side and wants to become a pastor himself. He said the conservative Christian movement has not weakened. "We're still voting our values. We're not saying vote Republican or vote Democrat. We're saying vote." Cheryl Rieser, a Columbus kindergarten teacher and mother of two who has been an educator for 12 years, is worried about the way the government is headed. In schools, the trend to avoid Christian influences forces teachers to be "really careful."

## Taking off the Gloves

"It's almost like if you talk about Christianity, you have to do it with kid gloves. It's our basis and our heritage, yet when you teach history, they want you to dance around it." Rieser, a survey respondent who attends Hope Assembly of God of Groveport, said she could not vote for a candidate who wasn't opposed to abortion rights. She also believes politicians should be open about their religious views. "Anything that is going to touch their voting is something that's open for our view," she said. "I need to know how a person is going to vote, because I want to vote my values." Leonard Mapes, of the Stark County city of Alliance, said it's right for clergy members to express political opinions but not to tell congregates how to vote. "I think there's this misunderstanding about clergymen, pastors, ministers. . . . They vote, too. They should be able to express themselves openly. . . . They are leaders of a group of people." Mapes is a 63-year-old retired director of credit for Sears who attends a nondenominational church. He has been a minister part time for 30 years. "My Christian influence does play a big role in my thinking when I go in that booth," he said.

## Voting for God

Mapes talks to people about voting and current issues and frequently writes letters to politicians, from Bush on down. He rarely gets a reply, even though he's made significant contributions to the Republican Party in Ohio and nationally. "I'm voting because it's my God-given right. I'd feel like a traitor to my own county if I didn't vote."

Sandra Tapp, 46, a fine-arts framer from Cuyahoga Falls, near Akron, said it's appropriate for ministers to offer religious advice to politicians and congregates. "God's in charge of everything. . . . If the pastor or ministers are in tune to God, they're going to influence people."

Tapp left the Catholic church for 26 years before rejoining recently.

"As much as I can, I apply my biblical beliefs. It's not up to us any more," Tapp said. "God's in charge. God has a plan. "If I vote in line with his will and his ways, in the big picture he's going to win and we're going to win."

## EVALUATING THE AUTHORS' ARGUMENTS:

The viewpoint you just read quoted people who strongly believe that Christians should be politically involved. Did these Christians cite the Bible or other religious authorities to support their views? Does that matter? Why or why not?

# Christianity Is Not Meant to Resolve Political Disputes

## Darryl Hart

*"The basic teachings of Christianity are virtually useless for resolving America's political disputes."*

Darryl Hart argues in this viewpoint that Christianity is not suited to resolving political disputes. He says that Christianity historically is intolerant of views that conflict with dogma and that Christianity has little to say about what public policy should be. He says Christianity's essential purpose is spiritual, not temporal, and mixing Christianity with politics trivializes faith. Hart is the author of A Secular Faith: Why Christianity Favors the Separation of Church and State, from which this viewpoint is excerpted.

**AS YOU READ, CONSIDER THE FOLLOWING QUESTIONS:**
1. Whom does the author say is considered more of an oddity today, the Religious Right or people without belief?
2. Who does the author say "cheapened Jesus" by declaring June 11, 2000, "Jesus Day"?
3. How does the author compare the work of the church and the duties of citizenship?

Darryl Hart, *A Secular Faith: Why Christianity Favors the Separation of Church and State.* Chicago: Ivan R. Dee, 2006. Copyright © 2006 by Darryl Hart. All rights reserved. Courtesy of Ivan R. Dee, Publisher.

*Controversy over prayer in the classroom has led to many legal battles.*

enerally speaking the attitude of secular elites has changed dramatically from twenty-five years ago, when the fundamentalists in Jerry Falwell's Moral Majority seemed a scary intrusion of conservative faith into partisan politics. . . .

So acceptable has religion become because of its presence in American politics that people without belief, not the Religious Right [a U.S. political faction advocating social and religious conservatism], may be the real oddity.

## Christianity Is Intolerant

Still, before traditional Christians become too comfortable with the idea that faith is normal, they may consider two important reasons for being suspicious of the current friendliness to religion in public life. The first is that the apologists for faith-based politics appear to be incapable of recognizing that Christianity has historically been an exclusive and intolerant faith. In other words, because conservative Christians opposed deviance from received truth, a brief for Christian-friendly politics is inherently incompatible with a polity that includes a variety of faiths. . . .

## Christianity Does Not Address Public Policy

The second reason to be suspicious of the recent openness to religion in public life is that the estimates of specifically Christian contributions to American politics may in fact be dead wrong about the Christian religion. As great an intellectual and practical problem as it is to distill the good generic qualities of the world's religions from a particular faith's less attractive teachings and practices, this [essay] . . . is not about this specific difficulty. Instead it is about Christianity in the United States, and more about Protestantism than Roman Catholicism because of the former's larger involvement in and responsibility for the political developments of American society. . . . Christianity in its classic formulations, especially the Protestant traditions of Lutheran, Reformed and Anglican, has very little to say about politics or the ordering of society. This does not mean that Christianity has nothing to say. Clearly, certain notions about men and women being created in the image of God, or about the sinfulness of human nature, or even about the legitimacy of personal property, have implications for politics. But beyond these implications, which may be applied in a variety of ways, Christianity has little to say explicitly about the sort of polity in which Americans have been living for the last 230 years. In fact, when Christians have tried to establish a Christian basis for the planks of political party platforms, or even for broad-based social reforms, they have fundamentally misconstrued their religion. . . .

## Christianity Will Not Solve Political Problems

What does Christianity require of its adherents politically? In applying this question to the relationship between faith and politics, rather than asking how much religion a liberal democracy can comfortably tolerate, the subject looks decidedly different. At the very least it requires some knowledge, first, of the religious meaning of Christianity. Once you clear this hurdle, negotiating America's political order looks like a piece of cake. This isn't to say

> **FAST FACT**
>
> A Pew Research Center poll from 2006 found that 63 percent of Americans believe the will of the people, not the Bible, should have more influence over the law of the country.

# Religious Affiliation of the 110th Congress

| Religion | Number in House | Number in Senate | Percent of Congress | Percent of Population |
|---|---|---|---|---|
| AME (v) | 2 | 0 | 0.4 | (u) |
| Anglican | 1 | 0 | 0.2 | (w) |
| Assembly of God | 4 | 0 | 0.7 | 0.5 |
| Baptist | 60 | 7 | 12.5 | 16.3 |
| Buddhist | 2 | 0 | 0.4 | (y) |
| Christian (x) | 16 | 2 | 3.4 | 6.8 |
| Christian Reformed | 2 | 0 | 0.4 | (y) |
| Christian Scientist | 5 | 0 | 0.9 | 0.1 |
| Church of Christ | 1 | 1 | 0.4 | (y) |
| Church of God | 0 | 1 | 0.2 | 0.5 |
| Congregationalist | 0 | 1 | 0.2 | (z) |
| Congregation - Baptist | 1 | 0 | 0.2 | (u) |
| Disciples of Christ | 2 | 0 | 0.4 | 0.2 |
| Eastern Orthodox | 4 | 1 | 0.9 | 0.3 |
| Episcopalian | 27 | 10 | 6.9 | 1.7 |
| Evangelical | 2 | 0 | 0.4 | 0.5 |
| Evangelical Lutheran | 1 | 0 | 0.2 | (u) |
| Evangelical Methodist | 1 | 0 | 0.2 | (u) |
| Hindu | 0 | 0 | 0.0 | 0.4 |
| Jewish | 30 | 13 | 8.0 | 1.3 |
| LDS (Mormon) | 10 | 5 | 2.8 | 1.3 |
| Reorganized LDS | 1 | 0 | 0.2 | (u) |
| Lutheran | 14 | 3 | 3.2 | 4.6 |
| Methodist | 48 | 13 | 11.4 | 6.8 |
| Muslim | 1 | 0 | 0.2 | 0.5 |
| (Church of) Nazarene | 1 | 0 | 0.2 | 0.3 |
| Presbyterian | 35 | 9 | 8.2 | 2.7 |
| Protestant (x) | 22 | 4 | 4.9 | 2.2 |
| Quaker | 1 | 0 | 0.2 | 0.1 |
| Roman Catholic | 130 | 25 | 29.0 | 24.5 |
| Seventh-day Adventist | 2 | 0 | 0.4 | 0.3 |
| Unitarian | 1 | 1 | 0.4 | 0.3 |
| United Church of Christ | 2 | 4 | 1.1 | 0.7 |
| Unaffiliated | 6 | 6 | 1.1 | 14.1 |

(u) No discreet category exists in the
    American Religious Identification Survey
(v) African Methodist Episcopal
(w) Included with Episcopalians
(x) No denomination stated
(y) Less than 0.05 percent
(z) Included with United Church of Christ

Taken from: The Pew Research Center for the People & the Press that mastering Christianity 101 will solve America's political and cultural contests. It will not. My argument is that the basic teachings of Christianity are virtually useless for resolving America's political disputes, thus significantly reducing, if not eliminating, the dilemma of how to relate Christianity and American politics.

## Politics Trivializes Faith

Too often in considerations of religion and American politics, Christianity has been misunderstood. But, more important, where Christians have tried to use their faith for political engagement they have generally distorted Christianity. The editors of the *New Republic* captured part of the distortion that attends politicized Christianity when they wrote of then Texas governor George W. Bush's decision to make June 11, 2000, Jesus Day, a holiday dedicated to Christ's example of "love, compassion, sacrifice, and service." An editorial in the magazine suggested that Bush did not glorify but "cheapened Jesus," because the reason for Christ's specialness is not simply his contribution to social service but his status as the second person of the Trinity. Attempts to employ the sacred and eternal for the common and temporal end up trivializing faith, which is "the certain fate of religion in the public square.". . .

## Kingdom Not of This World

Christianity is essentially a spiritual and eternal faith, one occupied with a world to come rather than the passing and temporal affairs of this world. . . .

I want those advocates of Christianity's public role and political responsibility to take seriously Jesus Christ's own words when he said, "My kingdom is not of this world." At one time in American history, sixty or so years ago, evangelical Protestants knew that those words involved an ambivalence about the rulers and principalities of this world. Now otherworldliness seems a fossil of an older time when faith knew its place. This is why not only evangelicals but Christianity's political allies must consider the otherworldly implications of the Christian religion. . . .

## Two Different Vocations

The love of God, tenacity about worship, defensiveness about sacred rites, aversion to false religion—all are parts of genuine faith that make it impractical if not damaging for public life. The downside of religion in American politics is that the demands of public life tame Christianity's deeper significance and make it conform to standards alien to faith. . . .

A fundamental difference exists between the work the church is called to do in proclaiming the messages of Christianity and the vocations to which church members are called as citizens.

## EVALUATING THE AUTHOR'S ARGUMENTS:

The author of the article you just read argues that the teachings of Christianity cannot provide guidance for public policy. Do you agree? Why or why not?

# Wealth Is a Goal of Christianity

### John W. Adams

*"Poverty is a sickness and an indication of a conscious separation from God."*

In this viewpoint, John W. Adams, an ordained Unity minister and director of Golden Key Ministry–Unity, argues that prosperity is a proper goal of Christianity. He argues that God wants people to be rich and that Jesus said people had a right to prosperity. He says everyone should do everything possible to become prosperous. The key, Adams believes, is for people to have a positive view of money and it will to flow into their lives.

**AS YOU READ, CONSIDER THE FOLLOWING QUESTIONS:**

1. What does the author say was the view of Jesus regarding poverty?
2. Why, according to the author, did Jesus say there would always be poor people?
3. What, according to the author, is "God's green energy"?

I t is right for everyone, especially *you to* be rich! You should be just as rich as you possibly can. Unfortunately and ignorantly, some people do not believe this due to fear-based religious or parental training.

# Christianity and Money

*Christians were asked: How much influence do the following have on your thinking about money/finance?*

Respondents who stated "...a great deal."

| Influence | Total Christians | Protestant | Roman Catholic | Male | Female |
|---|---|---|---|---|---|
| Family/Spouse | 50% | 52% | 46% | 55% | 46% |
| Bible | 39% | 47% | 18% | 36% | 42% |
| Own Pastor/Religious Leader | 17% | 18% | 12% | 15% | 18% |
| Professional Financial Advisor | 15% | 14% | 14% | 13% | 16% |
| Religious leaders whose books you have read | 7% | 7% | 5% | 8% | 7% |
| Magazines/Newspapers | 7% | 6% | 9% | 6% | 8% |
| Religious leaders who you have seen on TV | 5% | 5% | 5% | 5% | 5% |
| Non-religious TV or radio personality who comments on personal finance | 4% | 4% | 4% | 4% | 3% |

Taken from: 2006 Poll, *Time Magazine*.

Regardless of what you may have been taught God wants you to be rich; to enjoy the happy, prosperous life and to do so in an honest way. You should be financially independent so that you may enjoy the good things money can provide, and because it is divinely right for you to be rich.

Granted, money is not everything, so *don't* make a god of it. Money doesn't . . . guarantee happiness, but having plenty of money does make it easier to have peace of mind, free you to be constructively creative, and to enjoy living in the manner to which you, and many others, want to be accustomed to.

## Money Is Good

It is far better to have plenty of money than to have less. Money is good. It is God's good green energy! Check up on your attitude towards money. If you have held negative thoughts about it, change them. They are not really valid and seriously impede your cash-flow. Improve your attitude toward money and more of it will flow more freely into your life!

> **FAST FACT**
>
> A *Time* magazine poll showed that 61 percent of Christians believe that God wants people to be financially prosperous.

Money responds to your thoughts about it, and the words you connect to it. Think and speak in an upward, positive way about money. Do not waste your good thought-energy thinking negatively about it. Do not fear it, or the having of too much money. Ask for wisdom and understanding, and affirm that money is coming to you now from every direction. Right now, you have the wisdom and intelligence to use money wisely and lovingly. . . .

It is wise to focus your energy upon your creative ability than to make money the object of your quest. Money will flow when you think right about it and work within and without to express your creative potential in prospering activity. Rather than being a motivator, let money be a barometer.

Be happy and grateful for the money you have had, have now, and expect to have. Declare that it is flowing into your life in abundant measure now. Pray this positive, prospering prayer:

"Money is good. It is flowing ever-increasingly into my life now.

I use it with wisdom and lovingly pass it on as it blesses me and all humankind. Thank You, God. I am grateful."

## You Have No Right to be Poor

Poverty is a sickness and an indication of a conscious separation from God, the Source. When there is such a separation in regard to wealth, there is usually a separation in regard to other aspects of living, as well. Conscious oneness with God is to be sought after and experienced on a continuing basis. God is within and all around you as the source of all that you are, can have, and experience. You cannot be separate from God except in consciousness.

Jesus never condoned poverty. He never decreed that anyone should be poor, although He acknowledged that the poor would always be around. He said this in recognition of the fact that some people wouldn't learn to use prosperity laws and principles.

*Many Christians have grown cynical after being defrauded out of millions of dollars by fellow church members.*

He did everything He could to convince people to claim, accept and enjoy their rightful inheritance of prosperous living as the deserving children of a loving and infinitely rich Father. He clearly taught and demonstrated "the life more abundant." And, He said "go and do likewise." Thus he gave you and me and everyone the authority to live the prosperous life.

Make no excuse for or put up with lack, at least as a permanent condition in your life. Do everything you can, inwardly and outwardly, to eliminate lack from your mind and your life, and to establish yourself in abundance.

## Prosperity at Its Best

Your loving Father-God intends for you to live in a gracious and successful manner. His desire for you is to experience now, daily good health, happiness, peace of mind, harmonious human relationships, and financial abundance. That is true prosperous living—prosperity at its best!

God has given you everything needed for living the prosperous life. Best of all, He has given you free choice and the *power of your spoken word.* Choose wisely!

You and I and everyone should do everything we can to claim and accept our rightful heritage of prosperous living, and to help others do the same.

### EVALUATING THE AUTHOR'S ARGUMENTS:

The author of the preceding viewpoint quotes Jesus as recommending a "life more abundant" and interprets this to mean monetary wealth. Can this phrase be interpreted in other ways? How so?

# Wealth Is Not a Goal of Christianity

## Patrick McCormick

Patrick McCormick argues in this viewpoint that Christ did not promote material wealth, but spiritual wealth. He says the "prosperity gospel" is not new, and is a moneymaker for those who preach it. McCormick believes that both the Old and New Testaments warn against the attraction of wealth, which makes people indifferent to the poor and is contrary to the message of Christ. McCormick is a professor of Christian ethics at Gonzaga University.

*"The Good News Jesus proclaimed to the poor was not a summons to wealth and prosperity but to sharing and compassion."*

**AS YOU READ, CONSIDER THE FOLLOWING QUESTIONS:**
1. How many people view the Rev. Creflo Dollar's TV show on the prosperity gospel, according to the author?
2. According to the author's interpretation of the biblical books of Amos, Isaiah, and Jeremiah, how did the wealthy acquire their riches?
3. What does Jesus say, according to the author, about the effect of wealth on one's ability to enter the kingdom of heaven?

Patrick McCormick, "Finance Ministers: 'Prosperity Gospel' Preachers Claim to Know the Good News—and for a Nominal Fee, You Can Have it, Too," *U.S. Catholic,* vol. 72, January 2007, pp. 42-43. Copyright © 2007 by Claretian Publications. Reproduced by permission.

W hen Jesus began his public ministry in Luke 4:18, he announced he had been sent to "preach Good News to the poor." According to a small but growing number of today's televangelists and megachurch pastors [leaders of large, independent, nondenominational Christian congregations], the Good News Jesus came to proclaim is that God means for all of us to be rich—or at least very prosperous.

Advocates of the increasingly popular "prosperity gospel" argue that the faithful have but to ask God for an abundance of spiritual and material blessings, and they will be showered with a bounty of health, wealth, and success in their various endeavors. Of course these blessings will be more abundant for those who place their faith in Jesus and render a healthy tithe to the collection plate.

## Prosperous Preachers

The Rev. Creflo A. Dollar Jr. has been preaching this "prosperity gospel" for two decades, and if the overflowing congregations and collection plates at his Atlanta-based megachurch are any indication, the message is selling like hotcakes. Begun in a local grade school cafeteria back in 1986, his World Changers Church now boasts a membership roll of over 25,000 and an annual operating budget of more than $80 million. Moreover, Dollar's Changing Your World television show claims to reach a worldwide audience of 1 billion people, and for the past two years the apostle of prosperity has been preaching the gospel of success to sellout crowds at Madison Square Garden, raising $345,000 a month in tithings and donations.

Nor can anyone say that the good reverend doesn't practice the prosperity gospel he preaches. For while Jesus said, "the Son of Man has no place to lay his head," Dollar owns—among other things—a multimillion dollar home in Atlanta, a $2.5 million apartment in Manhattan's tony Time Warner Center, two Rolls Royces, and a private jet. It's easy to see why people would accept his invitation to "Come, follow me."

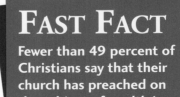

## FAST FACT

Fewer than 49 percent of Christians say that their church has preached on the subject of wealth in the last year, according to a 2006 *Time* magazine poll.

*Sisters of the Missionaries of Charity are among many orders of clergy who take a vow of poverty so they may help those less fortunate live healthy lives.*

## Prosperity Gospel Not New

The "prosperity gospel" may seem like good news to a large number of Christians in search of their piece of the American dream, but it is not exactly new news. Religious historians note that back in the 1950s radio and TV evangelists like Oral Roberts (and his Expect a Miracle show) were preaching the prosperity gospel to the same working- and middle-class audiences watching Queen for a Day.

Twenty years later New York's Rev. Ike was sending the gospel of success over the airwaves to 1,500 television and radio stations throughout the land. And a decade later Jim and Tammy Faye Bakker had built an entertainment empire selling the good news of prosperity to folks all over America. Then came the Bakker and Jimmy Swaggart scandals, and all of a sudden prosperous preachers seemed tacky and tasteless.

Still, you can't keep good news down, and in the last several years the Rev. Dollar has been joined by a variety of other apostles of prosperity. Popular evangelists preaching the gospel of God-helps-those-who-help-themselves (and tithe regularly) include the likes of Frederick Price, Joyce Meyer, Benny Hinn, and Joel Osteen, pastor of America's largest megachurch and author of the religious self-help bestseller *Your Best Life Now: 7 Steps to Living at Your Full Potential* (Faithwords). And any visit to your local bookstore reveals stacks of tomes preaching the self-help gospel of prosperity and success. America is bullish on the gospel of prosperity, in no small part because the gospel of prosperity baptizes our quest for the American dream of wealth and success. . . .

But is this really the Good News Jesus had in mind?

## Is Prosperity the Goal?

In Exodus and Deuteronomy God promised to deliver the Hebrews from poverty and slavery, leading them into "a land flowing with milk and honey," a land in which there would be no poor in their midst. But, as the prophets reminded the Israelites time and time again, God's blessings and bounty would only be showered on those who showed mercy and compassion to the poor and the outcast. The God of Israel loved and protected the widow, the orphan, and the stranger, and the righteous or holy Hebrew must practice God's liberating and compassionate justice to the poor.

But according to Amos, Isaiah, and Jeremiah, the wealthy and prosperous were often unjust, having accumulated their riches by coveting and stealing the lands and crops of the poor, by cheating the widow and alien in the marketplace, or by driving peasant farmers into crippling debt and slavery. And prosperity itself was regularly described as a spiritual illness, anesthetizing the consciences of the rich, making the wealthy deaf to the cries of the poor.

## What Did Jesus Say?

Indeed, when Jesus reads the scroll from Isaiah in Luke 4:18, the Good News he proclaims for the poor is a liberation from all the injustices imposed by the wealthy and prosperous. In the reign of God all the

## Survey of Christians' Views on Religion and Money

| | Total Christians | Protestant | Roman Catholic |
|---|---|---|---|
| God is not interested in how rich/poor you are | 86% | 85% | 87% |
| Christians in America don't do enough for the poor | 49% | 52% | 45% |
| Jesus was not rich and we should follow his example | 48% | 48% | 49% |
| Poverty can be a blessing from God | 45% | 47% | 41% |
| Giving away 10% of income is minimum God expects | 39% | 47% | 18% |
| If you give away money to God, God will bless you with more money | 31% | 32% | 21% |
| If you earn a lot of money you should give most away and live modestly | 30% | 31% | 30% |
| Material wealth is a sign of God's blessing | 21% | 21% | 21% |
| If you pray enough, God will give you money you ask for | 13% | 13% | 12% |
| Poverty is a sign that God is unhappy with something in your life | 7% | 6% | 7% |

Taken from: 2006 poll, *Time* magazine.

debts holding the poor in bondage will be forgiven, and anyone hoping to enter that kingdom of God must cancel the debts of the poor and release the bonds of the slave.

Like the prophets, Jesus is suspicious of the attractions and addictions of wealth, and he, too, warns that the hunger for prosperity will deafen our ears to the cries of beggars like Lazarus. According to Jesus the wealthy will find it hard indeed to enter God's reign, and the advice he gives the rich young man still sends chills through our hearts 2,000 years later.

Evangelists preaching the "prosperity gospel" get the Good News half right. The Bible reveals a loving God ready to shower mercy (and milk and honey) upon the poor and eager to liberate them from enslaving debt. But scripture also warns that wealth and prosperity are not signs of salvation in a world where 2 billion of our global neighbors live on less than $2 a day and where 800 million go to bed hungry every night. The Good News Jesus proclaimed to the poor was not a summons to wealth and prosperity but to sharing and compassion.

## EVALUATING THE AUTHOR'S ARGUMENTS:

The author of this viewpoint takes a view completely opposite to that in the previous article. Which view do you think is more correct? Give reasons for your answer.

# Christianity Is Under Attack

## Mark R. Rushdoony

*"Humanists are out to replace the rule of God with the rule of man."*

Mark R. Rushdoony argues in this viewpoint that humanists are enemies of Christianity and are trying to remove God from every facet of life. He says that humanism is a worldview that cannot coexist with Christianity. He argues that Christians must present a Christian worldview in all facets of life to win this cultural war. Rushdoony is president of the Chalcedon Foundation.

**AS YOU READ, CONSIDER THE FOLLOWING QUESTIONS:**

1. What examples does the author give to prove there are "wicked strategies" to remove God from U.S. culture?
2. What does the author say is the attitude of humanists toward God?
3. At the end of the article, what audience does the author say needs to be educated about the Christian worldview?

I f you're intellectually sensitive to the presuppositions underlying current events, you've already seen the explicit agenda of humanists to silence the Christian voice in America.

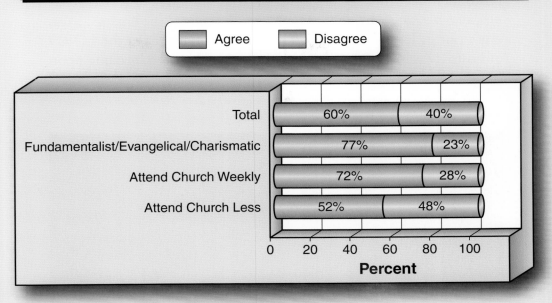

## Poll Shows Most Americans Think Christianity Is Under Attack

Agree  Disagree

| | Agree | Disagree |
|---|---|---|
| Total | 60% | 40% |
| Fundamentalist/Evangelical/Charismatic | 77% | 23% |
| Attend Church Weekly | 72% | 28% |
| Attend Church Less | 52% | 48% |

0   20   40   60   80   100
**Percent**

Taken from: Anti-Defamation League poll, October 2005.

No doubt you are greatly disturbed by the efforts of secularists, pluralists, and false religious groups to remove the Judeo-Christian God "from every post and pillar." The following is just a few of the wicked strategies imposed by such humanist organizations as the American Civil Liberties Union [ACLU], Americans United for the Separation of Church and State, and other secular and false religious groups:

- The persecution of Chief Justice Roy Moore in Alabama [who refused to remove a monument of the Ten Commandments from the courthouse]
- The judicial attempts to remove Christian symbols, such as the nativity, from every public place
- The elimination of public prayer from every local and federal institution
- The promotion of gay marriage in Massachusetts and San Francisco
- The unhindered encroachment of Islam throughout Western nations

These devices of the enemies of the Cross are the antithesis to the postmillennial prophecy of Zechariah who saw a day in which "*holiness unto the Lord*" shall be engraved "on the bells of the horses. . . Yea, every pot in Jerusalem and Judah shall be holiness unto the LORD of hosts" (Zech. 14:20–21). God's intent is to write His name upon

*Paul Mirecki of Lawrence, Kansas, is a victim of religious violence. He was attacked because of his plan to teach Intelligent Design at the local college.*

every area of life. The intention of humanistic man is to erase God's name from every area of life. In this generation, the battle lines are drawn! . . .

## Enemies of God

What do humanism, secularism, and Islam share in common? They are all religious worldviews. They all represent religious presuppositions whether their god is man or Allah. They are comprehensive systems of thought that speak to every area of life. A humanist is not content to simply retain his secularism within his own heart. He wants to impose his system on others within the public sphere. A Muslim never speaks of merely having a "personal relationship with Allah." Why? Because Islam is not a "religion of the heart." It is a worldview that commands every area of life and thought. . . .

Even though most mainstream evangelicals are angered by contemporary Christian persecution, they do not understand the nature of the conflict. For many, it is merely another assault by the camp of unbelievers. For others, the efforts of humanists and false religious groups seem more sophisticated and determined than in previous decades. Instinctively, evangelicals are realizing that they are dealing with an intellectually advanced opponent. . . .

## Replacing the Rule of God

In factuality, we are dealing with what both Cornelius Van Til and my father, R.J. Rushdoony, referred to as epistemological self-consciousness. This phrase is actually a very simple idea. Epistemology is the theory of knowledge. It means that when someone is epistemologically self-conscious, he is fully aware of the implications of his knowledge. He knows who and what he is and works tirelessly to fulfill the implications of his worldview in every area of life. In this sense, in order for the humanists to be consistent with their "knowledge" they must seek to erase God from every facet of life.

In a 1967 *Chalcedon Report* article my father wrote, "The humanists religiously deny every authority other than man, and their totalitarian state is a deliberately conceived man-god defying the order of God with man's own order." This is an accurate description of our present dilemma as Christians. Humanists are out to replace the rule of God with the rule of man.

However, humanism cannot progress by itself. Secularists can only advance by the mutual indifference of the Church. My father wrote,

"Today the impotence and confusion of humanism is marked. It is wallowing in failure all over the world, in failure, but not in defeat, because there is no consistent Christian force to challenge and overthrow it."

One might ask, "haven't Christians tried to oppose such groups as the ACLU?" Sure they have. The tools of opposition, however, have been limited. It requires much more than activism, evangelism, or revivalism to stem the tide of advancing humanism. Dad saw Christian education as central to strengthening Christian resistance:

"The intensely powerful religious force of humanism, with all its hatred of God and God's world law and order, can never be defeated by people whose ground of operation is vaguely Christian and largely humanistic. The lack of Christian episte-mological self-consciousness is one of the major reasons, if not perhaps the major, for the growing victory of the enemy."

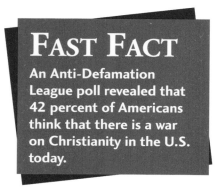

## FAST FACT

An Anti-Defamation League poll revealed that 42 percent of Americans think that there is a war on Christianity in the U.S. today.

## Workers for Christian Worldview

It's the lack of an articulated Christian world and life view that allows humanists to gain the high ground in the cultural war. This is why the single most important task of a Christian ministry is to educate and equip the believer with a comprehensive faith that speaks to all areas of life.

"It is therefore of the utmost importance for Christians to develop epistemological self-consciousness This means Christian educa-tion. It means a Christian philosophy for every sphere of human endeavor."

My father had a clear view of the social problems we face today. He also knew the answer: Christian education. This is why, more than ever, the work of Chalcedon must continue to influence not only its constituency, but a greater audience among mainstream evangelicalism. Simply stated, we've been "preaching to the choir" for too long. It's time to take our message to new frontiers.

## EVALUATING THE AUTHOR'S ARGUMENTS:

The author of this viewpoint says humanists seek to erase God from life. How does the author define a "humanist"? Would it include all persons who are not Christians? Could it include some Christians?

# Extreme Christians Are Attacking Freedom

## Alex Koppelman

*"These people don't want you to be able to live your life the way you want to lead it."*

Alex Koppelman argues in this viewpoint that instead of there being an attack on Christianity, it is extreme Christianity that is attacking individual freedom. The author says that evangelical Christians want to make their interpretation of religion a law that all must follow. Koppelman says Americans must protect their freedoms from this assault by extremists. Koppelman is a contributor to the *Daily Pennsylvanian*.

**AS YOU READ, CONSIDER THE FOLLOWING QUESTIONS:**
1. What examples does the author give of Christianity being a force for good in modern times?
2. What politician does the author quote as an example of Christian extremism?
3. When, does the author think, the cultureal war will be over?

Alex Koppelman, "Culture War Under Way in U.S.," *Daily Pennsylvanian*, April 21, 2005. Reproduced by permission.

T here's a battle going on for the soul of the United States. Don't believe me? Just ask Bill O'Reilly [the conservative political commentator], who came out and said it in his syndicated column this January, writing that there is a "culture war raging throughout the USA" and blaming it on "secular forces that see any Christian public display as an affront." Or ask [former, conservative] House Majority Leader Tom DeLay, who wrote in a letter to the Traditional Values Coalition that "for the last 40 years, the anti-Christian left in America has waged a sustained attack against faith in God, traditional moral norms, the rule of law and the traditional marriage-based family."

## Christian Extremists Started the War

O'Reilly and DeLay are right about one thing: There is undoubtedly a cultural war taking place in the United States, one that will have repercussions for generations to come. But it was not started by godless liberals, as they would have you believe. It was started by a group of extremists who want the world created in their image and who are becoming more influential by the day.

In the semester I have spent writing this column I have been accused, in comments on dailypennsylvanian.com and in a Jan. 19 [2005] column by Jennifer Weiss, of being anti-Christian. That is not the case. Indeed, I believe that Christianity has often been a force for good in modern times. Christians led the civil rights movement; they are at the forefront of many of the country's major charities. Many are led by their faith to wonderful acts of kindness and compassion. I attended a Quaker school for 14 years, and I saw there the incredible power that Christianity can have to change the world for the better.

## Opposing Freedom

My problem is with the forces of evangelical Christianity, ever more prevalent in the highest levels of government and media, that are seeking to remake this country as a theocracy. These people don't want you to be able to live your life the way you want to lead it;

## FAST FACT

A Pew Research Center poll showed 76 percent of Americans think posting the Ten Commandments on government property should be legal.

*The debate over teaching Intelligent Design in high school classrooms has led to fierce fighting over freedom of religion in public school systems.*

they don't want you to have access to anything they personally disapprove of. They don't want your children to learn about evolution, and all too many of them don't want your children to learn that homosexuals might be people, too.

In a column entitled "Suicide by Secularism?" which ran in *The Washington Post* on . . . Sunday [April 17, 2005], conservative columnist George Will wrote about what he perceives as an increasing secularity that threatens the very survival of Europe and the United States.

"The challenge confronting the church can be expressed in one word: modernity," he wrote. "The church preaches that freedom is life lived in conformity to God's will as manifested in revelation and interpreted by the church. Modernity teaches that freedom is the sovereignty of the individual's will—personal volition that is spontaneous, unconditioned, inviolable and self-legitimizing."

Will hit the nail on the head. The "culture war" being fought in the United States may seem like a series of unconnected battles over abortion rights, homosexual marriage and what we can or can't watch

## Poll Shows Mixed Feelings on Religion in Government

### Religion and Politics

| Have Liberals Gone Too Far . . . | | |
|---|---|---|
| In trying to keep religion out of schools and government? | | |
| | 2005 | 2006 |
| Yes | 67% | 69% |
| No | 28% | 26% |
| Don't know | 5% | 5% |

| Have Conservatives Gone Too Far . . . | | |
|---|---|---|
| In trying to impose their religious values on the country? | | |
| | 2005 | 2006 |
| Yes | 45% | 49% |
| No | 45% | 43% |
| Don't know | 10% | 8% |

### Parties' Attitudes Toward Religion

| The Republican Party is . . . | | |
|---|---|---|
| | 2005 | 2006 |
| Friendly | 55% | 47% |
| Neutral | 23% | 28% |
| Unfriendly | 9% | 13% |
| Don't know | 13% | 12% |

| The Democratic Party is . . . | | |
|---|---|---|
| | 2005 | 2006 |
| Friendly | 29% | 26% |
| Neutral | 38% | 42% |
| Unfriendly | 20% | 20% |
| Don't know | 13% | 12% |

Taken from: Pew Forum on Religion and Public Life, August 2006.

on television. But in the end, the fight comes down to two sides, and the choice is black and white. Eventually, we will all be asked to make the same choice the inhabitants of countries ruled by Islamic law once were: Do we believe that we should be allowed to act as free people, or do we believe that a particular religion's interpretation of God's law should dictate our daily life?

## We Must Protect Freedoms
Evidence that the war is raging is all around us. We can see it in our schools, where the scientific theory of evolution by natural selec-tion, the veracity of which only a few fringe scientists dispute, is

under attack by people who argue that in the interests of fairness and balance, the Christian story of creation must be taught as well. The creation stories of the thousands of other world religions are, of course, ignored. We can see it in our media, where a fight against "indecency" in broadcasting is slowly stripping us of the freedom to see even movies like "Saving Private Ryan" on TV because of the complaints of a small but active minority. We can see it in the new NBC miniseries "Revelations," which depicts scientists as unwilling to look for God and doctors as dark, ominous forces seeking to take the life of an instrument of God whose physical state is remarkably similar to Terri Schiavo's before her death.

This culture war has not abated, and it seems increasingly likely that it will not until every demand of this extremist fringe is met. It's up to the rest of us not to retreat as our freedoms are taken away.

## EVALUATING THE AUTHOR'S ARGUMENTS:

After reading this viewpoint and the one preceding it, do you see any points on which the authors agree? Explain your answer.

# Chapter 2

# What Is the Role of Gender and Sexuality in Christianity?

# Priests Must Be Celibate

## Pat Stratford

*"[Celibacy] is an imitation of the celibate Jesus, motivated by love of Him."*

In the following viewpoint, Pat Stratford argues that celibacy imitates the celibacy of Christ and has many values relevant to Christianity. He says there were never public complaints about celibacy until the sexual revolution changed modern culture. He claims that controversy over celibacy is part of a decline in morality that undermines marriage and promotes divorce, cohabitation, and single motherhood. Father Stratford is parish priest of Sandgate-Brighton in the Brisbane Archdiocese.

**AS YOU READ, CONSIDER THE FOLLOWING QUESTIONS:**
1. What type of sin does the author believe that celibacy expiates?
2. According to the author, what was the recommendation of the Second Vatican Council regarding celibacy for priests?
3. How long does the author say the Catholic Church has had a tradition of celibate priests?

Guided only by the secular press over the last 30 years, many young men could have come to believe that priests in general are unhappy in their vocation and resentful of their celibacy. We priests need to show by word and example that we are in fact happy in our vocation to the priesthood.

Pat Stratford, "Why the Church Must Continue to Uphold Priestly Celibacy," *AD2000,* vol. 20, February 2007, p. 20. Reproduced by permission.

*Chastity is one of the vows that new priests must accept upon ordination by the Catholic Church.*

The Second Vatican Council recommended celibacy for priests (*Ministry and Life of Priests,* par 16) and in 2004 the bishops from many countries around the world rejected the idea of changing the law on celibacy for priests. Should this be surprising?

While the number of ordinations to the diocesan priesthood has been on the increase in many parts of the world since 1978, the year John Paul II became Pope, at the same time, vocations have decreased in the West. Why has this occurred?

Two sociological factors should be recognised. First, the sharp decline in priestly vocations has coincided with a decline in the numbers of marriages and a rise in the levels of divorce, cohabitation and single motherhood. Second, these trends, which emerged in the 1960s, are characteristic of contemporary Western culture.

I was ordained in 1958 and for nearly ten years after that there were no public complaints about celibacy from priests. Then it began—coinciding with the sexual revolution—much to the delight of the secular media. Priests who left to get married received front-page coverage in some daily newspapers.

In fact, the so-called crisis of priestly celibacy is really a crisis of all forms of lifelong intimate commitment in marriage, priesthood and religious life. The cultural forces attacking celibacy are the same ones undermining and devaluing marriage.

The Christian community should not give way to this cultural onslaught. We need celibate priests, for they are ordained to offer sacrifice: not their own sacrifice, but that of Christ. A priest is a minister to the eternal sacrifice of Christ, a ministry which extends outwards from that core to the ministry of the word and sacraments. He is, in a general way, representative of God to people and of people to God. In that context, celibacy has many values.

Several years ago Fr Seamus Murphy SJ made the following points about the value of celibacy.

- Celibacy expresses the Church's belief in the truth of the New Testament, since it accepts the example and teaching of the Lord Jesus and St Paul that celibacy is positive and life-giving.
- It expresses the priest's own faith in the gospel and his personal trust in Jesus. In committing himself to celibacy, he is putting himself on the line, staking a most important part of his life on the call of Christ.
- It is a significant form of acceptance of Jesus' call to total renunciation for the sake of the gospel. The Christian community is always in need of people who will respond to that call.
- It is an imitation of the celibate Jesus, motivated by love of Him. It represents an acceptance of the idea that the priest must, as far as possible, be like the Master.
- It is sacrificial. It is a sharing in the sacrifice Jesus made through his life and death, as described in the Letter to the Hebrews

2:9-18 and 5:1-10. It is a way of living out Romans 12:1-2, where Paul appeals to the Roman Christians to involve their bodies in their sacrifice to God, going against the norms of the dominant culture.

- It is an expiation for sin, particularly sexual sin. In our time, when the sexual sins of clergy and religious are highlighted, it would be a serious mistake to drop celibacy, since it would amount to abandoning hope that abstinence is possible.
- It is a badly needed counter-witness to the sexual exploitation and irresponsibility, and contempt for sexual self-discipline, promoted by a consumer culture.
- It expresses solidarity with those who are fated, despite their desires, never to marry or have children.
- It is a counter-witness to the collapse of belief in permanent commitment, whether marriage or celibacy. It expresses belief in: (a) the possibility and (b) the value of lifelong celibacy. If the Church appears to give up on the possibility of lifelong celibacy, it will weaken the cultural support for lifelong marriage.

These values are very important, and the Church ought not risk giving the impression of watering them down. Given the contemporary culture, a decision to drop the celibacy requirement, going against 1,600 years of tradition, would inevitably be seen as undermining those values.

## EVALUATING THE AUTHOR'S ARGUMENTS:

The viewpoint you just read argues that celibacy imitates Christ. Does this mean that persons who are celibate are better persons or more spiritual than those who are not? Give reasons for your answer.

# Priests Should Be Allowed to Marry

## Emmanuel Milingo

*"A married priest is a healthier priest."*

Emmanuel Milingo argues that celibacy requirements have caused a shortage of priests. He argues that celibacy is not for everyone and marriage is more important than celibacy. Milingo says the loneliness of celibacy causes alcoholism, sexual misconduct, and other problems for priests. He claims that permitting priests to marry will help them identify with the families in their church and that parishioners want married priests. Milingo is an archbishop of the Catholic Church in Zambia.

**AS YOU READ, CONSIDER THE FOLLOWING QUESTIONS:**
1. According to the author, what notable married priests have been leaders of the church?
2. Why have a number of churches been closed, according to the author?
3. How does the author think marriage affects our relationship with God?

Emmanuel Milingo, "Press Statement: The Holy Spirit is Creating a New Church for a New Day," *Married Priests Now!*, November 28, 2006. Reproduced by permission.

On November 16th [2006], Pope Benedict XVI called a rare meeting of his cabinet, the Roman Curia, to specifically discuss the issues raised by our [Married Priests Now!] Prelature's call for a married priesthood in the Latin Rite of the Roman Catholic Church. His official cabinet includes twenty Cardinals who head the Vatican governmental offices, known as dicasteries.

## Celibacy Is Not for All

I, Archbishop Emmanuel Milingo, and the Married Priests Now! Prelature agree with the Holy Father and the Vatican in their statement that reaffirmed celibacy. We believe celibacy is a charism [a power given by the Holy Spirit] for some priests but not for all. The priesthood must be freed from celibacy as an obligation. Celibacy should be viewed as an option rather than the norm, a charism that is freely chosen, and not enforced as a job requirement. To continue to require celibacy as a prerequisite for ordination only exacerbates an already deteriorating and hemorrhaging situation within the Roman priesthood. Not every priest has the particular calling to be celibate and this is the problem.

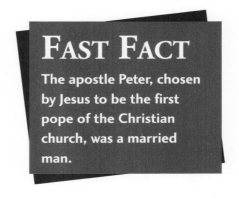

**FAST FACT**

The apostle Peter, chosen by Jesus to be the first pope of the Christian church, was a married man.

We do not believe that a meeting of the Cardinals who head the dicasteries [central offices of stewardship within the Roman Curia] was called to simply reaffirm celibacy. The report that was *not* released by the Vatican is the important one. What did the Cardinals actually say about a married priesthood? Is the Vatican in such a state of denial that it cannot see the need for a married priesthood?

## Celibacy Requirements Harm the Church

What, so far, has celibacy done for the church? On the American scene it has undermined the church by an ever-increasing sexual abuse scandal that has ruined the lives of countless young victims. It has cast a dark shadow of doubt on the holiness of the priesthood. The faithful can no longer trust their priests. The cost of celibacy has driven diocese

# Optional Celibacy Survey Results

Survey results by diocese of priests responding to the question: *Do you favor an open discussion of the mandatory celibacy rule for diocesan priests?*

| Diocese | Priests Responding | Yes | No | Unsure |
|---|---|---|---|---|
| Albany | 69 of 243 [28%] | 62% | 35% | 3% |
| Baltimore | 93 of 238 [39%] | 65% | 32% | 3% |
| Belleville | 55 of 159 [35%] | 71% | 25% | 4% |
| Boston | 321 of 1524 [21%] | 66% | 28% | 5% |
| Buffalo | 162 of 550 [29%] | 66% | 23% | 11% |
| Cincinnati | 174 of 542 [32%] | 67% | 29% | 4% |
| Cleveland | 114 of 500 [23%] | 64% | 32% | 4% |
| Columbus | 83 of 238 [35%] | 60% | 36% | 4% |
| Covington | 34 of 93 [37%] | 53% | 47% | 0% |
| Detroit | 160 of 768 [21%] | 70% | 24% | 2% |
| Denver | 78 of 292 [27%] | 58% | 37% | 5% |
| Dubuque | 101 of 222 [45%] | 56% | 40% | 4% |
| El Paso | 29 of 104 [28%] | 72% | 17% | 10% |
| Fall River | 78 of 237 [34%] | 65% | 26% | 8% |
| Fort Wayne-South Bend | 28 of 109 [26%] | 36% | 64% | 0% |
| Fort Worth | 40 of 109 [36%] | 60% | 30% | 10% |
| Fresno | 34 of 114 [30%] | 56% | 41% | 3% |
| Gallup | 15 of 85 [18%] | 60% | 40% | 0% |
| Gaylord | 15 of 78 [19%] | 67% | 27% | 7% |
| Grand Rapids | 30 of 135 [22%] | 61% | 35% | 0% |
| Green Bay | 106 of 329 [32%] | 77% | 21% | 2% |
| Harrisburg | 19 of 91 [21%] | 32% | 63% | 5% |
| Indianapolis | 51 of 166 [31%] | 84% | 16% | 0% |
| Kalamazoo | 16 of 69 [23%] | 38% | 50% | 13% |
| LaCrosse | 93 of 223 [42%] | 55% | 42% | 3% |
| Lansing | 49 of 185 [26%] | 68% | 26% | 4% |
| Las Cruces | 24 of 75 [32%] | 76% | 12% | 8% |
| Las Vegas | 23 of 77 [30%] | 87% | 13% | 0% |
| Los Angeles | 121 of 965 [13%] | 70% | 23% | 4% |
| Madison | 81 of 162 [50%] | 62% | 30% | 7% |
| Marquette | 13 of 101 [13%] | 50% | 31% | 0% |
| Monterey | 42 of 134 [31%] | 57% | 40% | 2% |
| Oakland | 126 of 301 [42%] | 84% | 13% | 2% |
| Oklahoma City | 46 of 121 [38%] | 57% | 39% | 4% |
| Orange | 40 of 164 [24%] | 68% | 25% | 8% |
| Paterson, NJ | 77 of 299 [26%] | 74% | 23% | 3% |
| Philadelphia | 128 of 900 [14%] | 47% | 50% | 3% |
| Phoenix | 100 of 304 [33%] | 77% | 19% | 4% |
| Providence | 123 of 400 [31%] | 51% | 46% | 2% |
| Pueblo | 26 of 84 [31%] | 69% | 23% | 8% |
| Raleigh | 44 of 155 [ 29%] | 79% | 16% | 5% |
| Rochester | 102 of 294 [35%] | 69% | 22% | 10% |
| Sacramento | 66 of 215 [31%] | 73% | 24% | 3% |
| Saginaw | 29 of 120 [24%] | 77% | 16% | 0% |
| San Bernardino | 62 of 258 [24%] | 75% | 17% | 6% |
| San Diego | 71 of 329 [22%] | 73% | 24% | 3% |
| San Francisco | 104 of 319 [33%] | 68% | 26% | 6% |
| San Jose | 66 of 184 [36%] | 70% | 23% | 8% |
| Santa Fe | 75 of 203 [37%] | 68% | 31% | 1% |
| Seattle | 68 of 290 [23%] | 79% | 16% | 4% |
| Steubenville | 30 of 57 [53%] | 57% | 40% | 3% |
| Stockton | 23 of 72 [32%] | 48% | 48% | 4% |
| Superior | 50 of 89 [56%] | 67% | 33% | 2% |
| Syracuse | 132 of 312 [42%] | 73% | 20% | 6% |
| Toledo | 78 of 210 [37%] | 77% | 22% | 1% |
| Tucson | 64 of 193 [33%] | 70% | 27% | 3% |
| Venice | 51 of 164 [31%] | 73% | 18% | 10% |

Taken from: http://futurechurch.org/fpmsurvey/index.htm

*Lack of numbers among the clergy may lead the Catholic Church to listen to proponents of allowing priests to marry.*

after diocese into bankruptcy and church properties have been sold to pay off claims of sexual misconduct by priests. Celibacy, because of its loneliness and lack of intimacy has helped turn thousands of priests into alcoholics.

The Vatican's denial of the problem confirms and encourages our mission to recall married priests to full active ministry within the Roman Catholic Church. The Married Priests Now! Prelature is the only Catholic diocese calling for the ordination of married men and for the return of married priests to full ministry.

## Marriage Trumps Celibacy

Marriage is a sacrament of the church, celibacy is not. Marriage is a higher calling than celibacy. The marriage vow trumps the celibacy promise. Our Prelature believes that a married priest is a healthier priest, and that a married priesthood will give priests a wholesome and proper outlet for their sexuality. We are created by God as sexual beings and our sexuality needs to be celebrated as a blessing for ourselves and our wives. Marriage needs to be the normal option for priests. Remember that Jesus called married priests first. St. Peter was a married priest. The New Testament priesthood was a married priesthood. It is time for the Roman Catholic Church to return the gift of the married priesthood to the Latin Rite.

The sanctity of the church is in the family. The holiness of marriage and family reflects the community of love that we find in the Trinity. The love of the Father, Son and Holy Spirit is the true model of the holiness of the family. Marriage brings us closer to God. A married priesthood can create wonderful families that because of marriage will identify more closely with the families they serve in the church and community. It will foster equality for women in the church and bring a new form of democracy in church management.

## Groundswell for Married Priests

There is sadness in the Church over the dire situation caused by the shortage of priests. The faithful realize that they are not being well served because the priests who remain are elderly, clearly over-extended and cannot meet the needs of the faithful. Hundreds of churches have been closed and laymen and laywomen are being appointed as pastors of churches. The faithful see and feel the problem and often do reach out to the married priests who are available and willing to meet their spiritual demands. This is a groundswell movement—a church within a church—that is forming and the Vatican is in a state of denial. Our Prelature is part of this movement. This is a New Pentecost.

The Holy Spirit is creating a new church for a new day. . . . We are the Voice of All Suffering Catholics, the Voice of the True Church, calling on the Vatican to be attentive to the needs of its faithful people. We ask all of the Roman Catholic faithful to join us in prayer for this New Pentecost. Let your voices also be heard loudly and clearly in Rome and in your home dioceses. Let the bishops know that you want married priests now. Recalling married priests is a wholesome and simple remedy to help save the church. Pray that the married priests will be reinstated to full active ministry and that married men will be called to the priesthood.

## EVALUATING THE AUTHOR'S ARGUMENTS:

The author of this viewpoint claims that marriage is more important than celibacy. The author of the previous viewpoint argued that the opposite is true. After reading both viewpoints, which position do you think is more beneficial for parishioners—that priests be married or that they remain celibate? What are the advantages and disadvantages of each?

**Viewpoint**

**3**

# Women Should Be Ordained as Priests

## Angela Bonavoglia

*"It's clear that women have been ordained."*

In the following viewpoint, Angela Bonavoglia argues that the Catholic Church's refusal to ordain women as priests is sexist. She says arguments that the tradition requiring only men to be priests is dishonest because women have been ordained in the past and at least one bishop was a woman. She argues that the public now supports ordaining women priests. Bonavoglia is the author of *Good Catholic Girls: How Women Are Leading the Fight to Change the Church*.

**AS YOU READ, CONSIDER THE FOLLOWING QUESTIONS:**
1. Whom does the author claim was a female bishop?
2. Whom does the author say was a female apostle recognized in the Epistle of Paul to the Romans?
3. As reported by the author, what billboard advertisement did the Women's Ordination Conference mount in 2000?

Angela Bonavoglia, I Will Disobey this Unjust Law," Salon.com, July 31, 2006. This article first appeared in Salon.com at http://www.salon.com. An online version remains in the Salon archives. Reprinted with permission.

By their visibility and accessibility, a small band of women are forcing a confrontation. They are asking, Is sexism a sin? How does the church reconcile its teaching that women and men are created in God's image, that once baptized, there is "no male or female" and "all are one in Christ Jesus," with its contention that women cannot represent the ultimate sacred or hold ultimate power through ordination because they are, literally, the wrong "substance"? The statement from the Diocese of Pittsburgh condemning the ordinations asserted this argument against women's ordination: that priests must resemble Jesus physically. That belief is based, in part, on the notion of the substance of a sacrament: in the case of the Eucharist, bread and wine; and of holy orders, a man. Comparing people to food, the press release said: "Just as a priest cannot consecrate the Eucharist if he uses something other than unleavened white bread and wine from grapes, so too a bishop cannot confer Holy Orders on anyone other than a baptized man.". . ..

## Illicit Ordinations

The Roman Catholic womenpriests movement came into public view on June 29, 2002, when seven women were ordained priests on the river Danube between Austria and Germany, out of any bishops' clear jurisdiction. Presiding was the controversial Argentine Bishop Romulo Antonio Braschi. Though no longer in good standing with Rome, he had been ordained a bishop and could therefore provide the apostolic succession required for ordination. In church speak, the new women priests consider themselves ordained validly but illicitly (because of canon law). Within two months, the Congregation for the Doctrine of the Faith, headed by then Cardinal Joseph Ratzinger, now [Pope] Benedict XVI, excommunicated all seven women and publicly chastised them for having "wounded" the church.

That action did nothing to quell the movement, which advocates "a new model of priestly ministry," a servant rather than an imperial priesthood, and seeks no break from Rome. In the years since the first ordinations—as Muslim women have boldly led prayer services and the first female bishop has risen to head the U.S. Episcopal Church— another 32 women (including today's 12) have been ordained Catholic deacons or priests, and 120 more are in training. These events have taken place on the Saone River near Lyon, France; Lake Constance between Germany and Switzerland; the St. Lawrence, between the United States and Canada; and in Barcelona, Spain. Secret "catacomb" ordinations have been held, too. . . .

## Worldwide Women's Movement

In fact, the womenpriests movement did not spring out of whole cloth but has its roots in the worldwide movement for women's ordination in the Catholic Church. The women who launched the U.S. movement in the 1970s were energized—as are women today—by the legendary "Philadelphia 11," who in 1974 forced open the doors of the priesthood in the U.S. Episcopal Church. They were "irregularly" ordained by retired and resigned Episcopal bishops, an action that resulted in the denomination's approval of women's ordination the following year.

As I've traveled around the country talking with women about the church, why they stay, what they love, what they're fighting to change, invariably a woman—sometimes young, most of the time older— will rise and share her great dismay at the thought of women priests. Indeed, the Catholic Church is steeped in a rich sacramental tradition, and some cannot separate that tradition from the men who have claimed to exclusively represent it. But that has been changing. While in the 1970s, 29 percent of Catholics supported women's ordination, today some 60 percent do. In addition, as Peter Steinfels, author of "A People Adrift: The Crisis in the Roman Catholic Church in America," explains, "the burden of proof has shifted." It used to be that advocates had to explain why women should be priests; today, the hierarchy has to explain why not.

## Women in the Early Church

Frankly, in attempting to defend the church's ban on women's ordination, Catholic spokespeople sound a little like used-car salesmen. They have a lot full of old models. You don't like this argument? No problem. What about the one over there? The Last Supper used to anchor a central argument. There, the teaching holds, Jesus commissioned the 12 male apostles to be the only leaders of his church, from whom all other leaders, male too, had to proceed. The idea of ordination came much later. The problem is, no one knows who was at that Passover meal. And, as theologian Elizabeth Johnson once said in a lecture, do we really think that Jesus, who was so welcoming to women followers, decided that night to leave all the women, including his mother, out in the cold? To which I would add another question: If women were allowed at the meal (which they had probably prepared), then when Jesus said over the bread and wine, "Do this in remembrance of me," did he also say, "only you guys"?

The hierarchy insists that the church has a constant tradition of ordaining only men. But what about Junia the apostle and Phoebe the deacon, in the Epistle of St. Paul to Romans? What about those tomb inscriptions for "Leta *presbitera*" and "Guilia Runa, woman priest"? What about Bishop Theodora, über-apostle Mary Magdalene, and

*Unauthorized ordinations of women within the Catholic Church are becoming more frequent as numbers among the clergy decline.*

Ludmila Javorova, who is still alive? In 1970, the late Bishop Felix Davidek ordained Javorova as a Catholic priest to serve in the underground church in communist-occupied Czechoslovakia, which she did until communism fell and the Vatican banned her ministry.

## Women Have Been Ordained

Here things get really sticky, with the church fathers essentially declaring that when applied to women, "apostle" doesn't mean apostle, "bishop" doesn't mean bishop, "priest" doesn't mean priest, "deacon" doesn't mean deacon, and "ordained" doesn't mean ordained. They, in fact, turned Junia into Junias, a man, until theologian Bernadette Brooton restored her to her rightful gender, and they dismiss the others as "wives of." Says Kathleen Strack, who has a master's degree in divinity and will be ordained a priest today, "The emperor has no clothes. It's clear that women have been ordained. Is [what the hierarchy does] a deliberate lie? Is it that no one remembers? I don't know, but they continue to perpetuate a falsehood."

Not surprisingly, church spokespeople vigorously denounce the movement for women's ordination. William Donahue of the Catholic League has dismissed the ordained women out of hand and declared their supporters to be "mad feminists" from "the asylum." In an e-mail response to my specific questions, director of communications Robert Lockwood called the rich concrete evidence of women's ordination "archaeological myth-making of the *Da Vinci Code* variety" and "hardly relevant.". . .

## Sign from God

Despite all of the hierarchy's protestations, the threats, the silencing, the firings, the expulsions and the excommunicating, the conversation goes on. And the women priests keep coming, giving Catholics a new representation of the divine. I'm reminded of an action by the Women's Ordination Conference [WOC] back in 2000, in response to a million-dollar campaign by the Archdiocese of Chicago to recruit more priests. The diocese mounted a billboard announcing its campaign, and WOC mounted a dueling billboard. Hung over a major highway in Chicago, WOC's billboard read: "You're waiting for a sign from God? This is it. Ordain women."

**EVALUATING THE AUTHOR'S ARGUMENTS:**

The author argues that treating women and men differently in the church is sexist. Do you agree with her argument? Why or why not? What reasons, if any, could justify confining persons to roles in the Catholic Church based on gender?

# Women Should Not Be Ordained as Priests

## Donna O'Conner

*"The Pope does not have authority to change the rules governing priestly ordination."*

Donna O'Conner argues in this viewpoint that gender inequality has nothing to do with restricting priesthood to men. She says women cannot be ordained as priests because it was not what Jesus willed. For this reason, she says, the pope lacks authority to confer ordination on women. She claims that allowing women to perform priestly functions is heresy. She argues that women who seek ordination simply want a different religion than the one established by Jesus. O'Conner writes for *Catholic Insight*.

**AS YOU READ, CONSIDER THE FOLLOWING QUESTIONS:**
1. According to the author, when did discussion of women's ordination between proponents and the Church begin to take place?
2. What did the Council of Nicea state in A.D. 315 regarding women deacons?
3. How does the author view attempts to use feminist language in scripture translations?

Donna O'Conner, "The 'ordination' of 'womenpriests'," *Catholic Insight*, October 1, 2005. Copyright 2005 *Catholic Insight*. Reproduced by permission.

## Statistics on Women Clergy

| Denomination | Ordination of Women Permitted? | Percent Women Clergy |
|---|---|---|
| Catholic | No | 0% |
| Eastern Orthodox | No | 0% |
| Episcopalian | Yes, beginning in 1976 | 21% |
| Evangelical Lutheran Church in America (ELCA) | Yes, beginning in 1970 | 13% |
| Lutheran-Missouri Synod | No | 0% |
| Methodist | Yes, beginning in 1956 | 19% |
| Latter-day Saints (Mormon) | No | 0% |
| Presbyterian Church (USA) | Yes, beginning in 1956 | 20% |
| Southern Baptist | No | 0% |
| Unitarian Universalist | Yes, beginning in 1863 | 60% |
| Islam | No | 0% |
| Judaism (Conservative) | Yes, beginning in 1985 | 11% |
| Judaism (Orthodox) | No | 0% |
| Judaism (Reform) | Yes, beginning in 1972 | 16% |

Taken from: Beliefnet.com, 2007 (www.beliefnet.com/womenclergychart.html).

From July 22–24, 2005, the second Women's Ordination Conference took place in Ottawa [Canada]. It concluded with the so-called ordination of four "priestesses" and five "deaconesses" on the St. Lawrence River [between the United States and Canada]. As the Catholic archbishops of Kingston and Ottawa explained, the event had nothing to do with the Catholic Church.

The media thought it did. They spoke of possible excommunications. They praised the women for being "reformers" of the Catholic Church, of being "sincere" and "courageous." They spoke of "Catholic" women being involved in the Catholic Church, but they were wrong.

In 2002 the "Womenpriest" movement "ordained" seven Catholic women. [The church hierarchy in] Rome excommunicated them and told them they were no longer members of the Catholic Church. That was the first and also the final excommunication. Consequently, the

2003 "ordination" of three Womenbishops, the further ordinations on the Danube and the Saone (France) rivers in 2004, and the July 2005 ones on the St. Lawrence (seven Americans, one Canadian) were no concern of the Catholic Church, other than feeling regret about the foolishness of the affair and the evil of apostasy. . . .

Some added information with respect to their arguments. . . .

### Gender Inequality

The Church's decision in this matter has nothing to do with inequality and everything to do with Christ and the history of the Church. [Jesus] chose twelve male apostles and they are the foundation of His Church. In the second and third centuries, some people admitted women to at least some priestly functions, not ordination, and this was considered heresy. The response was that this was not what Christ willed, and against apostolic teaching.

The fact that the Blessed Virgin Mary, Mother of God and Mother of the Church, received neither the mission proper to the apostles nor the ministerial priesthood clearly shows that the non-admission

*Two thousand years of all-male priesthood has left many people feeling that women will never be equals in the Catholic Church.*

of women to priestly ordination cannot mean that women are of lesser dignity, nor can it be construed as a discrimination against them. . . .

## Pope Lacks Authority

Discussion of this matter has taken place between proponents of women's ordination, especially the Anglican church and the Secretariat of Christian Unity in Rome since the early 1970s. It has been thoroughly exhausted by every Pope since that time. Each one has tried in depth to explain the Church's position, the history behind it, and the fact that the

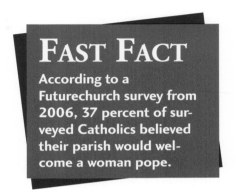

**FAST FACT**

According to a Futurechurch survey from 2006, 37 percent of surveyed Catholics believed their parish would welcome a woman pope.

Pope does not have the authority to change the rules governing priestly ordination to include women. After 25 years of debate Pope John Paul II wrote a final and definitive Apostolic Letter, Ordinatio Sacerdotalis, On Reserving Priestly Ordination to Men Alone. It stated: ". . . in order that all doubt may be removed in virtue of my ministry of confirming the brethren (cf. Lk 22:32) I declare that the Church has no authority whatsoever to confer priestly ordination on women and that this judgement is to be definitively held by all the Church's faithful. May 22, 1994."

Due to a number of problematic and negative statements from some organizations within the Church that followed Ordinatio Sacerdotalis, Joseph Cardinal Ratzinger, Prefect of the Congregation for the Doctrine of the Faith, wrote a reply, approved by John Paul II, and published in 1995. Part of it reads, "The teaching that the Church has no authority whatsoever to confer priestly ordination on women, which is presented in the Apostolic Letter, Ordinatio Sacerdotalis, is to be held definitively and is to be understood as belonging to the deposit of faith." It concluded, "This teaching requires definitive assent, since, founded on the written Word of God, and from the beginning constantly preserved and applied in the Tradition of the Church, it has been set forth infallibly by the ordinary and universal Magisterium during the Second Vatican Council, in the Dogmatic Constitution on the Church. Thus, in the present circumstances, the Roman Pontiff, exercising his proper office of confirming the brethren (cf. Lk 22:32), has handed on the same teaching by a formal declaration, explicitly stating what is to be held always, everywhere, and by all, as belonging to the deposit of the faith."

The position of the Church in this matter has been made abundantly clear, any further discussion would be meaningless and open to misinterpretation. . . .

## Women Deacons Were Never Ordained

There were deaconesses in the early Church, but they were not the female equivalent of deacons. The term comes from the Greek word meaning one who serves or helps. Women deaconesses brought Holy Communion to houses where a priest might not be admitted during the times of persecution. They also helped to anoint the naked bodies of women prior to baptism. Obviously the priest could not do this. When the persecutions were over and adult converts had become rare, the need for these women died away.

In the first Council of Nicea, 315, it was stated that women deacons were not ordained and were to be counted among the laity. . . .

## Feminist Language Distorts Dogma

The campaign for feminist language in scripture translations and in the liturgy has turned out to be a grave attack on the substance of the faith. Such alterations become awkward, unnatural, inconsistent and not inclusive. Father and Son are neutered to parent and child, and the Holy Spirit becomes feminine. However, Satan always remains masculine. Feminist language angers most people, and it even drives some from the Church. It turns the Sacrifice of the Mass into a political statement. Its worst effect is that it distorts revealed dogmas and it redefines Jesus' loving Father, our personal God, into an abstraction even more removed from us, until He, our God, becomes an impersonal, universal energy. The purpose of these language changes is to alter the meaning of the Scriptures and the message of the liturgy to make them compatible with feminist thinking. . . .

These women are not solely interested in ordination or finding a bishop to obey; they want a different church from that of Jesus Christ. They evangelize for practices borrowed from New Age spiritualism and they advocate ecclesiastical approval of non-celibate and women priests, divorce and remarriage, contraception, abortion, and homosexual activity. Unfortunately, many priests and laity do not understand that these women have left the Catholic Church both in spirit and in deed.

## EVALUATING THE AUTHOR'S ARGUMENTS:

Now that you have read opposing viewpoints on the issue of ordaining women as priests, how do the two authors differ in their recounting of Catholic Church history? How does this difference affect the credibility of each author's arguments?

# The Church Should Affirm Gay Marriage

**United Church of Christ, General Synod 25**

*"Theologically and biblically, there is [no] justification for denying any couple, regardless of gender, the blessings of the church. . ."*

In this excerpt from a resolution adopted by the United Church of Christ, the argument is made that the Bible's call for justice and compassion require the Christian Church to affirm equality of marriage rights regardless of gender. It is the covenantal relationship of trust, rather than the genders or sexuality of the parties, that is important. All people, regardless of sexual orientation, are made in the image of God, says the United Church of Christ, and ideas about marriage have changed over time.

**AS YOU READ, CONSIDER THE FOLLOWING QUESTIONS:**
1. According to the author, what marriage model does the Bible commend?
2. How many rights and benefits in federal statutes require legal marriage according to figures cited by the author?
3. What figure in the Bible does the author say radically challenged traditional cultural roles and concepts of family life?

"In Support of Equal Marriage Rights for All," *United Church of Christ, General Synod,* vol. 25, July 4, 2005. Reproduced by permission.

*"Beloved, let us love one another, because love is from God; everyone who loves is born of God and knows God."*

—1 John 4:7

*"Therefore what God has joined together, let no one separate."*

—Mark 10:9

Ideas about marriage have shifted and changed dramatically throughout human history, and such change continues even today. At different points marriage has been defined in response to economic realities, by the primacy of procreation and by societal understandings of the role of men and women. In the Gospel we find ground for a definition of marriage and family relationships based on affirmation of the full humanity of each partner, lived out in mutual care and respect for one another. Scripture itself, along with the global human

*Proponents of gay marriage within the Catholic faith have become more widespread.*

experience, offers many different views of family and how family is to be defined. This unfolding revelation and understanding needs to be weighed carefully by people of faith considering the issue of equal marriage rights for couples regardless of gender. Jesus radically challenged his traditional cultural roles and concepts of family life. Jesus boldly declared members of the household/family of God to be whoever hears and follows the will of God.

## Justice and Equality

Civil/legal marriage carries with it significant access to institutional support, rights and benefits. There are more than 1,400 such rights and benefits in the federal statutes alone. Efforts to ban civil marriage to couples based on gender denies them and their children access to these rights and benefits, and thus, undermines the civil liberties of these couples, putting them and their children at risk.

Throughout its history, the United Church of Christ [UCC] has been at the forefront in the struggle for justice and equality. For more than 30 years, the General Synod of the UCC has adopted resolutions affirming lesbian, gay, bisexual and transgender (LGBT) persons, consistently calling for an end to discrimination, equal protection under the law, deploring LGBT hate crimes and violence, supporting LGBT relationships and families, celebrating the gifts of LGBT persons for ministry and encouraging all settings of the church to be open and affirming of LGBT persons, welcoming them and encouraging their participation in every aspect of the mission and ministry of the church. . . .

## What the Bible Requires

The message of the Gospel is the lens through which the whole of scripture is to be interpreted. Love and compassion, justice and peace are at the very core of the life and ministry of Jesus. It is a message that always bends toward inclusion. The biblical story recounts the ways in which inclusion and welcome to God's community is ever-expanding—from the story of Abraham and Sarah, to the inclusive ministry of Jesus, to the baptism of Cornelius, to the missionary journeys of Paul throughout the Greco-Roman world. The liberating work of the Spirit as witnessed in the activities of Jesus' ministry has been to address the situations and structures of exclusion, injustice and oppression that diminish God's people and keep them from realizing the full gift of human personhood in the context of human communion.

The biblical call to justice and compassion (to love one's neighbor as one's self) provides the mandate for marriage equality. Justice as right relationship seeks both personal and communal well being. It is embodied in interpersonal relationships and institutional structures, including marriage. Justice seeks to eliminate marginalization for reasons of race, gender, sexual orientation or economic status.

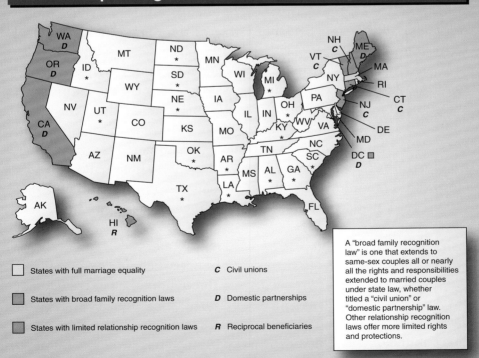

**Relationship Recognition for Same-Sex Couples in the U.S.**

☐ States with full marriage equality

☐ States with broad family recognition laws

☐ States with limited relationship recognition laws

*C* Civil unions

*D* Domestic partnerships

*R* Reciprocal beneficiaries

A "broad family recognition law" is one that extends to same-sex couples all or nearly all the rights and responsibilities extended to married couples under state law, whether titled a "civil union" or "domestic partnership" law. Other relationship recognition laws offer more limited rights and protections.

## Gospel Values of Covenant

The language of covenant is central to the message of scripture concerning relationships and community. Both in the message of the prophets and the teachings of Jesus, covenant relationships are important, taken seriously by God and are to be taken seriously by God's people. The overriding message of the Gospel is that God calls God's people to live fully the gift of love in responsible, faithful, just, committed, covenantal relationships of trust that recognize and respect the image of God in all people. These Gospel values are at the core of the covenantal relationship that we call marriage.

It is essential to note that the Gospel values of covenant do not come from the practices of marriage, which change and evolve throughout the history of the biblical story. Indeed, it is not possible to rely exclusively on scripture for understanding marriage today. For example, biblical texts that encourage celibacy, forbid divorce, or require women to be subservient to their husbands are not considered to be authoritative because they are primarily expressions of the cultural norms of the ancient Middle East. At the same time, there are also many biblical models for blessed relationships beyond one man and one woman. Indeed, scripture neither commends a single marriage model nor commands all to marry, but rather calls for love and justice in all relationships.

We recognize and affirm that the covenantal values that are essential to the Gospel are central to how we understand marriage in this time. We also recognize and affirm that all humans are made in the image and likeness of God, including people of all sexual orientations, and God has bestowed upon each one the gift of human sexuality. Further, we recognize and affirm that, as created in God's image and gifted by God with human sexuality, all people have the right to lead lives that express love, justice, mutuality, commitment, consent and pleasure.

## God Still Speaking About Marriage

Is God still speaking about marriage? The overwhelming testimonies of countless couples, regardless of gender, throughout the United Church of Christ, and beyond, say, "Yes, God is still speaking." Couples who have chosen to exchange covenantal vows attest to the blessing of God's abundance and life-giving power in their relationships. Through their committed relationships, many throughout the church—parents, siblings, children, friends and others—have witnessed the liberation of the gifts of God for service in the world.

Therefore, theologically and biblically, there is neither justification for denying any couple, regardless of gender, the blessings of the church nor for denying equal protection under the law in the granting of a civil marriage license, recognized and respected by all civil entities.

## EVALUATING THE AUTHOR'S ARGUMENTS:

The viewpoint you just read argues that love and compassion, peace and justice are more important than particular norms of sexuality, which change over time. Do you agree? Why or why not?

## Viewpoint 6

# The Church Should Oppose Gay Marriage

### The Research Institute, Southern Baptist Convention

*"Homosexual behavior is sinful and contrary to God's design."*

The Research Institute of the Southern Baptist Convention says in this viewpoint that the Christian Church must oppose gay marriage because the Bible teaches that homosexuality is sinful and homosexual behavior has negative physical, social, and spiritual consequences. The institute contends that homosexuals must abandon homosexual behavior and seek forgiveness from God. The author calls on churches to oppose gay marriage and support laws to ban it.

**AS YOU READ, CONSIDER THE FOLLOWING QUESTIONS:**
1. According to the author, what was God's design for marriage?
2. How, says the institute, does same-sex marriage weaken the family?
3. According to the author's interpretation of the Bible, how does God feel about homosexual behavior?

The Research Institute, Southern Baptist Convention, "Nashville Declaration on 'Same-Sex Marriage'," *For Faith and Family, Ethics & Religious Liberty Commission,* March 9, 2005. Reproduced by permission.

Across the country the American people have spoken loudly, clearly repudiating attempts to redefine marriage. In every state in which citizens have been given the opportunity, they have voted to reaffirm the historic definition of marriage as only the union of one man and one woman. Yet activist judges are still in a position to force so-called "same-sex marriage" on the American people, and have already shown a willingness to do so in a number of states. In response to the serious challenge to the traditional biblical definition of marriage, we are compelled to make the following declaration:

## One Man, One Woman

*1. We affirm the biblical teaching that God designed marriage as a lifetime union of one man and one woman. We deny that the God-ordained institution of marriage is subject to redefinition as merely a civil institution or simply a private matter.*

The *Baptist Faith and Message* declares: "Marriage is the uniting of one man and one woman in covenant commitment for a lifetime. It is God's unique gift to reveal the union between Christ and His church and to provide for the man and the woman in marriage the framework for intimate companionship, the channel of sexual expression according to biblical standards, and the means for procreation of the human race" (Article XVIII, "The Family").

**FAST FACT**

Seven states passed constitutional amendments banning gay marriage in 2006.

## Same-Sex Marriage Prohibited by Bible

*2. We affirm that marriage has certain essential defining personal and social characteristics. We deny that a same-sex relationship can ever be the same as or equivalent to marriage.*

The *Kansas City Declaration on Marriage* articulates many of the defining characteristics of the biblical concept of marriage:

- Marriage is the foundational institution of human culture (Genesis 2:18–22; Matt. 19:3–9; Eph. 5:22–33; Eph. 6:1; 1 Thess. 2:7, 11; 1 Tim. 5:4).

- Marriage is a covenantal relationship (Gen. 2:23–25; Mal. 2:14–16; Matt. 19:5–9; Eph. 5:31).
- Marriage creates one unity out of the two corresponding genders (Gen. 2:23–24; Matt. 19:4–6; Mark 10:6–9; 1 Cor. 6:16; Eph. 5:22–33).
- Marriage provides the best environment for the personal, social, and economic well-being of children (Eph. 5:22–33; Eph. 6:1; 1 Tim. 5:8; Titus 2:4–6).
- Marriage encourages the development of healthy sexual identity in children (Gen. 1:27–28; Gen. 2:18; Deut. 6:4–25; Prov. 1:8–9).
- Marriage is life-affirming (Gen. 1:27-28; Gen. 2:18; Prov. 5:18–19).
- Marriage is the only appropriate context for sexual relations (Lev. 18:22; Rom. 1:18–32; Heb. 13:4).
- Marriage is the ideal model for the family (Prov. 31:10–31; Eph. 5:22–33; Eph. 6:1–4; 1 Thess. 2:7, 11; 1 Tim. 3:1–7, 8–12; 1 Pet. 3:1–7).

## Same-Sex Marriage Harmful

On the other hand, inherent within "same-sex marriage" are significant harmful social consequences.

- "Same-sex marriage" undermines commitment to genuine marriage. Studies of the state of marriage in the Scandinavian countries that have legalized "same-sex marriage" reveal that traditional marriage has been adversely affected by the redefinition of marriage. In some Norwegian counties traditional marriage has practically disappeared.
- "Same-sex marriage" is detrimental to society. By undermining commitment to genuine marriage, "same-sex marriage" weakens the family, which is the foundational social institution of culture.
- "Same-sex marriage" is inadequate as a family context for children. It does not provide children with an opportunity to observe and understand the uniqueness of both sexes and to develop their own sexual identity in relationship to a father and a mother.
- "Same-sex marriage" is destructive personally. Homosexual behavior has negative physical, social, and spiritual consequences.

The *Resolution in Defense of Marriage* by the six Southern Baptist

*The belief that marriage should only exist between one man and one woman is strongly encouraged in church doctrine.*

Seminaries concludes, "Any legal recognition of same-sex relationships—whether known as 'marriages,' 'civil unions,' or any other nomenclature—is a direct act of defiance before God, and a rejection of God's perfect design for human sexuality, human relatedness, and the raising of children." We deplore "same-sex marriage" in the same way that we deplore any behavior that violates or compromises God's design for marriage.

## Homosexuality Is Sinful

*3. We affirm without reservation the biblical teaching that homosexual behavior is sinful and contrary to God's design. We deny the legitimacy of any attempt to characterize homosexuality as an acceptable or unchangeable alternative lifestyle.*

We agree with the *Colorado Statement on Biblical Sexual Morality* that "The Old and New Testaments uniformly condemn sexual contact between persons of the same sex (Lev. 18:22; 20:13; Rom. 1:26–27; 1 Cor. 6:9; 1 Tim. 1:10); and God has decreed that no one can ever excuse homosexual behavior by blaming his or her Creator (Gen. 2:24; Rom. 1:24–25)."

Scripture teaches that homosexual behavior is:

- Ungodly: "We know that the law is not meant for a righteous person, but for the lawless and rebellious, for the ungodly and sinful, for the unholy and irreverent, for those who kill their fathers and mothers, for murderers, for the sexually immoral and homosexuals, for kidnappers, liars, perjurers, and for whatever else is contrary to sound teaching. . . ."(1 Tim. 1:9–10, HCSB)
- Immoral: "Do not be deceived: no sexually immoral people, idolaters, adulterers, male prostitutes, homosexuals, thieves, greedy people, drunkards, revilers, or swindlers will inherit God's kingdom." (1 Cor. 6:9–10, HCSB)
- Dangerous: ". . . men with men committing indecent acts and receiving in their own persons the due penalty of their error." (Rom. 1:27, NASB)
- Unnatural: ". . . for their women exchanged the natural function for that which is unnatural, and in the same way also the men abandoned the natural function of the woman and burned in their desire toward one another." (Rom 1:26–27, NASB)
- Degrading: "Therefore, God delivered them over in the cravings of their hearts to sexual impurity, so that their bodies were degraded among themselves." (Rom. 1:24, HCSB)
- Repugnant: "You are not to sleep with a man as with a woman; it is detestable." (Lev. 18:22, HCSB)

## Homosexuals Need God's Forgiveness

Scripture also teaches that homosexuality does not have to be a permanent condition. Like any other sinful behavior, homosexual behavior can be forsaken, homosexual sin can be forgiven, and homosexual attractions can be changed. The Bible affirms that God can liberate anyone from homosexuality:

"Some of you were like this; but you were washed, you were

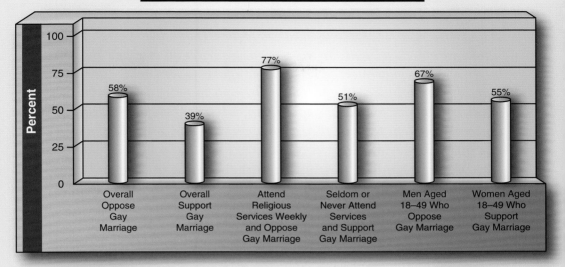

**2006 Gallup Poll on Gay Marriage**

| | Overall Oppose Gay Marriage | Overall Support Gay Marriage | Attend Religious Services Weekly and Oppose Gay Marriage | Seldom or Never Attend Services and Support Gay Marriage | Men Aged 18–49 Who Oppose Gay Marriage | Women Aged 18–49 Who Support Gay Marriage |
|---|---|---|---|---|---|---|
| Percent | 58% | 39% | 77% | 51% | 67% | 55% |

Source: Baptist Press, May 22, 2006 (http://www.bpnews.net/bpnews.asp?ID=23295).

sanctified, you were justified in the name of the Lord Jesus Christ and by the Spirit of our God." (1 Cor. 6:11, HCSB)

*4. We affirm that all people are created in the image of God and are of equal worth before God. Acknowledging that all of us are sinful and in need of God's forgiveness, we express our compassion for those trapped in homosexuality. We deny that God hates people who practice homosexual behavior.*

While the Bible clearly states God's abhorrence of homosexual behavior, it also clearly states His love for all human beings. God makes Christ's substitutionary death on the cross available to homosexuals in the same way that He offers it to anyone else, and He is as ready to redeem homosexuals as anyone else. We declare our love and concern for those trapped in homosexuality, and pledge to do all we can to assist those who desire to escape this destructive behavior to do so. We pledge ourselves to pray that God will give wisdom to our government and church leaders as they address the current debate over homosexuality and "same-sex marriage" in our nation in a compassionate way that affirms the worth of homosexual men and women but also encourages them to abandon homosexual behavior.

# Gay Marriage Must Be Opposed

*Therefore, because of the clear biblical teachings about homosexuality and marriage, and the serious social consequences that homosexuality and "same-sex marriage" pose for our nation, we reject all attempts to legitimize "same-sex marriage." The multiple efforts to legitimize "same-sex" marriage are misplaced and unwise attempts to redefine the historical, social, and moral foundation of human culture. Therefore, we urge all concerned citizens to resist these efforts with all due conviction, and we issue the following appeals:*

- We urge families to strengthen their bonds of love and commitment so that children have a better chance to develop God-honoring, healthy, appropriate sexual orientation.
- We urge Christians to educate themselves more adequately on the biblical teachings about homosexuality, marriage, and the serious social consequences of "same-sex marriage."
- We urge Christians to reach out to men and women trapped in homosexuality to provide them the relationships that will help them abandon homosexual behavior.
- We urge church leaders to help their congregations understand the biblical teaching on marriage and homosexuality.
- We urge churches to develop redemptive ministries of compassion to homosexuals that affirm their worth before God and that help them escape homosexuality.
- We urge all Christians to call on Congress to pass immediately an amendment to the U.S. Constitution defining marriage in the United States as the union of one man and one woman.

## EVALUATING THE AUTHOR'S ARGUMENTS:

The viewpoint you just read argues that God abhors homosexuality but loves homosexuals. Is there a contradiction between those two ideas? Why or why not?

# Chapter 3

# What Is the Future of Christianity?

*Many writers, such as Gershom Gorenberg (pictured here), believe that the apocalypse is just around the corner.*

**Viewpoint**

**1**

# Megachurch Worship Is the Future of Christianity

## Mark Chavez

Mark Chavez argues in this viewpoint that church membership is becoming concentrated in extremely large, nondenominational Protestant churches, known as megachurches. This trend, he says, exists in all denominations. The increased concentration is not the result of a steady growth of all churches, he says, but of very rapid growth by a few churches. The concentration of people and resources in large churches makes such churches more powerful politically and socially. Chavez teaches sociology at the University of Arizona.

> *"Every denomination shows the pattern of increased concentration from 1970 to the present with no end in sight."*

**AS YOU READ, CONSIDER THE FOLLOWING QUESTIONS:**
1. What percentage of people, money, and staff make up the largest 1 percent of Protestant churches, according to Chavez?

2. According to the author, what number of people, money, and full-time staff are concentrated in the largest 20 percent of churches?
3. How many Protestant churches in the United States have attendance of at least two thousand, according to statistics cited by the author?

M egachurches are increasingly difficult to ignore. By the latest count there are approximately 1,200 Protestant churches in the United States that have a weekly attendance of at least 2,000. The rise of megachurches raises the question: Why now? Why have very large churches proliferated in recent decades? Did something happen in the 1970s or 1980s to make the number of very large churches start to increase in those years?

With a lot of help from denomination-based researchers, interlibrary loan and dedicated students, I examined church size in 12 Protestant denominations back to about 1970, and over a longer period for seven of these denominations. Overall, I tracked the church-size distribution in American Protestantism from about 1900 to the present.

## More Large Protestant Churches

Three results stand out. First, across the Protestant spectrum, there are more very big churches. This increase might not be surprising in the case of growing denominations such as the Southern Baptist Convention and the Assemblies of God, but the same trend is evident

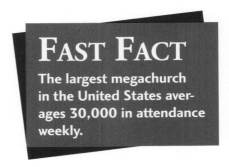

**FAST FACT**

The largest megachurch in the United States averages 30,000 in attendance weekly.

in denominations with declining membership over this period. The number of very large churches has increased, for example, in the Episcopal Church, the Evangelical Lutheran Church in America and the United Methodist Church. The number of very large Protestant churches has increased in almost every denomination on which we have data, and it does not matter whether the denomination is big or small, liberal or conservative, growing or declining.

The rate of increase in the number of very large churches seems to have picked up in the 1970s, but the trend toward more very big churches did not begin in that decade. For example, the number of Presbyterian churches with more than 2,000 members increased from 5 in 1900 to 74 in 1983. The number of Episcopal churches of that size increased from 7 in 1930 to 33 in 1960; for Missouri Synod Lutherans the number goes from 2 in 1900 to 23 in 1967. Conventional wisdom on this subject says that the number of very large churches has increased recently—and the results bear that out but conventional wisdom fails to recognize that this is not entirely a post-1970 trend.

The long-term nature of this trend suggests that simple population growth and increased population density are partly responsible for the proliferation of megachurches. If a town or city or suburb of a certain size is needed in order to support a 2,000-person church, then the more communities of that size there are, the more 2,000-person churches there will be.

## Big Churches Getting Bigger

A second observation is that the very biggest churches are getting bigger. This too is a long-term trend that did not begin in the 1970s, though again it seems that the rate at which the largest churches are getting bigger has accelerated since that decade.

A long-term trend of this sort could occur by a demographic process of growth proportional to size. If churches simply keep growing by means of births to current members, for example, then the biggest churches would constantly get bigger.

This simple demographic explanation doesn't work, however, because it assumes that yesterday's biggest churches would also be today's biggest churches. The biggest churches would be bigger than they were before, but the same churches would still be at the top of the heap. However, this is not the case.

## Rapid Growth of Some Churches

Yesterday's very biggest churches are not today's very biggest churches. Many of today's biggest churches grew very rapidly; their size is not the result of a steady, long-term increase. And this has been true for at least 100 years. Across all the denominations examined and across

*A stadium-sized church with a community of like-minded Christians may be the future of the Christian Church in the United States.*

the entire 20th century, the half-life of being one of the 20 biggest churches in a denomination is 20 to 30 years. That is, of the 20 biggest churches in a given year, only half of them will still be on that list 20 years later, only one-quarter still on the list 40 years later, and only two or three still on the list 60 years later.

It is not that these very large churches peak and then shrink dramatically, although some do. Rather, the biggest churches of the moment are overtaken by a new cohort of churches that have caught the latest cultural wave and ridden it to the top, and then those churches are overtaken by the next wave, and so on.

## Increased Concentration in Large Churches

The most interesting development, however, is a third trend: people are increasingly concentrated in the very largest churches. Most churches are small, but most church members are part of large congregations. The median church has fewer than 100 regular participants, but the median churchgoer attends a congregation with 400 regular partici-

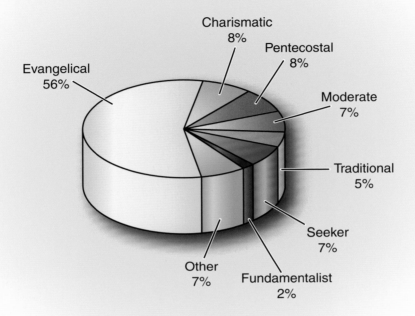

## Theology of Megachurch Congregations

Evangelical
56%

Charismatic
8%

Pentecostal
8%

Moderate
7%

Traditional
5%

Seeker
7%

Fundamentalist
2%

Other
7%

Taken from: Hartford Institute for Religion Research, *Megachurches Today 2005*.

pants. Even though there are relatively few large congregations, large congregations contain a disproportionate share of the churchgoing population. The biggest 1 percent of Protestant churches, for example, contain approximately 15 percent of all the people, money and staff. The biggest 20 percent of churches have between 60 and 65 percent of all the people, money and full-time staff.

You may have heard of the 20/80 rule of social life: 20 percent of the people do 80 percent of the work, 20 percent of the organizations control 80 percent of the resources, and so on. In Protestantism it's more like a 20/60 rule, but the basic phenomenon is the same. People and resources are heavily concentrated in the biggest churches. This has been true of American religion for a long time, but the level of concentration is increasing. . . .

Every denomination shows the pattern of increased concentration from 1970 to the present, with no end in sight. Denominations vary in how concentrated they are, but all of them show the same trend toward increasing concentration since about 1970. . . .

Each denomination on which we have data over the longer term was relatively highly concentrated before 1930, and concentration everywhere decreased until about 1970, after which it started to increase, again everywhere. . . . In every denomination on which we have data, people are becoming increasingly concentrated in the very largest churches, and this is true for small and large denominations, for conservative and liberal denominations, for growing and declining denominations.

## Social and Political Implications

This increased concentration may have social and political implications. Increased concentration of members makes religious institutions more visible, since one 2,000-person church is more visible—if only because of the size of its building—than ten 200-person churches. Increased concentration also increases the potential for social and political influence. Since one 2,000-person church is easier to mobilize for social or political action than ten 200-person churches, a politician is more likely to address one 2,000-person church than ten 200-person churches, and the pastor of one 2,000-person church probably gets an appointment with the mayor more easily than any of the ten pastors of the ten 200-person churches. Increasing concentration also affects intradenominational politics and the development and diffusion of worship practices. Also, increased concentration can create the illusion of religious revival when in fact it's the social organization of religion that has changed, not the overall level of religious participation or commitment.

## EVALUATING THE AUTHOR'S ARGUMENTS:

The author says that increased concentration of churches gives them more power to effect political and social change. If true, is this a good thing? Why or why not?

# Home Worship Is the Future of Christianity

**Lisa Smith**

In this viewpoint, Lisa Smith presents evidence that home worship could replace traditional institutional churches. She says home churches are attracting Christians in their 20s and 30s because such churches emphasize personal relationships. Fewer rules and routines also make home churches more attractive to younger Christians, she says. Smith writes for *Daily Herald* (Arlington Heights, IL).

*"Worship is about connection."*

## AS YOU READ, CONSIDER THE FOLLOWING QUESTIONS:

1. According to the author, how has the percentage of Americans attending home church weekly changed over the past decade?
2. According to the study cited by the author, members of megachurches consist largely of what demographic group?
3. What, according to experts quoted by the author, attendance growth rate is predicted for home churches during the coming decade?

There are no pews and no altar, just six chairs arranged in a circle.

There is no pastor relating Scripture to contemporary American life, just a group of friends discussing spirituality.

Neither bread nor wine is offered. Most who walk in are clutching cups of Starbucks coffee.

Yet the people who enter this Arlington Heights living room every Sunday morning label this gathering—and themselves—church.

"We have a deep conviction that we grow spiritually when we're in relationships," said Andy Padjen, 33, who has been hosting this weekly get-together for about the past year. "We feel like a lot of times there's some structure and theology in the institutional church that limit people's intimacy with each other. So we're all about making relationships central, helping people to be known and loved."

That's something that attracted Curtis Anderson to the group after a lifetime of involvement in traditional churches. Getting to know Padjen and the others in the group has made the Lake in the Hills resident feel closer to God.

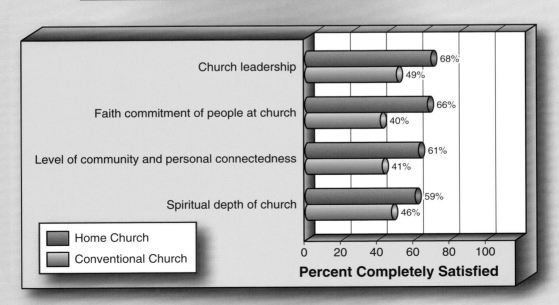

**Survey Shows Home Worship More Satisfying**

Church leadership — Home Church 68%, Conventional Church 49%

Faith commitment of people at church — Home Church 66%, Conventional Church 40%

Level of community and personal connectedness — Home Church 61%, Conventional Church 41%

Spiritual depth of church — Home Church 59%, Conventional Church 46%

Home Church
Conventional Church

0   20   40   60   80   100
**Percent Completely Satisfied**

Taken from: The Barna Group, Ltd., January 8, 2007.

"I would say that we would all agree that we're feeling God in a very personal way through the group," said Anderson, 29.

One of the reservations he had about abandoning traditional church life was that it wouldn't be as fulfilling. He's says that proved to be unfounded.

"I've been surprised at how it feels like it can be church," Anderson said. "It's definitely redefined (church) for me. This is the real thing."

Called a variety of terms including house or home church, organic church, and simple church, meetings like this are popping up across the country. Several prominent Christian authors believe they could replace traditional brick-and-mortar churches, especially if they continue to attract Christians in their 20s and 30s.

## Cultural Shift

Researcher and author George Barna said the house church trend shows Christians are moving away from the late 20th-century megachurch movement that made South Barrington's Willow Creek Community Church and others like it so popular.

A cultural shift is taking place, Barna argues. Some of the characteristics that made the megachurch attractive to baby boomers, such as elaborate worship performances in a concert-like venue, are what is driving away the next generation of Christians.

"If you look at the boomer generation, one of the values that drives that generation is size," Barna said.

His study, published in June, is based on interviews with more than 5,000 randomly selected adults from across the country.

"The issue of size shows why megachurches are a big deal," Barna said.

"You take boomers out of megachurches and you generally don't have a lot of people left."

Many children of baby boomers "see their parents gave up relationships to have money, and they see they're missing a significant dimension of life," he said.

> **FAST FACT**
>
> One out of five Americans attends a house church at least once a month, reports the Barna Group, Ltd.

In response, the younger generation places a high priority on establishing and maintaining relationships with one another, Barna said. They don't like the anonymity of a Protestant megachurch, he says.

About 9 percent of U.S. adults—20 million people—attend a house church on a weekly basis, according to Barna's research.

That number increased from just 1 percent of Americans a decade ago, and Barna predicts house church attendance will double in the coming decade.

"The culture is changing so substantially and relatively rapidly that most Americans—particularly the young—don't perceive a right way to do anything. There's a willingness to experiment with new forms of relationships," Barna said.

That's how it was with Padjen, who had always been a committed churchgoer until about a year ago. He was raised in an evangelical Christian home, attended a Christian college for four years and interned at Willow Creek while working on a master's degree in church leadership.

But he felt something was missing, he began to realize. Padjen and his roommate stopped going to church, and instead spent Sunday mornings praying for each other and holding intense spiritual discussions.

They invited others to join them. Now the group, which meets for two hours every Sunday, has grown to six people.

"We do a lot of listening to God together, spiritual exercises," said Padjen, a substitute teacher in Wheeling Township Elementary District 21. "And share. We kind of roll with that."

On a recent Sunday, each of the six, ranging in age from 29 to 46, jotted down their memories about past church group experiences, discussed their recollections and prayed for one another.

"One of the hallmarks of the house church phenomenon is that there are very few rules or routines that have to be followed," Barna said.

"Some streams in the house church community would say, 'That's part of the reason we're not a conventional church. Worship is not about routine. Worship is about connection.' They're not looking for a different meeting place so they can have the same agenda and activities you'd find in a conventional church."

## Traditional, too

At a house church in North Aurora, the weekly gathering consists of a short Bible study followed by a discussion on prophesy, some singing,

*Personalizing their faith is one aspect of why home-based worship continues to flourish within the Christian community.*

more Bible study, more singing and prayer. It resembles a traditional church service, save for the bread-maker humming on the kitchen island.

Aurora resident Dave Church leads the service. Since he co-founded this group six years ago with an Aurora couple, people have come and gone. Those who have left include the co-founding couple, Jim and Judy Larson, now missionaries trying to help prostitutes in Thailand.

Glenn Meisner, who hosts the church with his wife, Laurinda, echoes Padjen's statements about the house church's focus on relationships.

"Philosophically, the whole concept of a home fellowship, to me, inviting someone to a meeting isn't even the main thing," Glenn Meisner said. "It should be that we are pushing ourselves onto other people's worlds, getting involved with other people."

Those other people include students Meisner meets as a substitute teacher at West Aurora High School and drug-addicted residents of Aurora's Wayside Cross Ministries whom Church and Meisner meet during their monthly visits there. Many are invited to this house church.

The result is a multicultural, socioeconomically diverse group of 12 people who gathered at the Meisner home one recent morning: the home-schooled 12- and 15-year-old Meisner children, Church's Korean immigrant wife, a Wayside resident, a 16-year-old West Aurora sophomore, a 21-year-old West Aurora graduate, a Mexican couple with a baby, and an 11-year-old neighbor who is friends with the Meisners' younger daughter.

The Meisners found the idea of a home fellowship appealing after two churches they were members of moved from rented meeting spaces into expensive buildings.

"The focus was on getting that building going," Laurinda Meisner said. "We lost that fellowship. We lost the most important thing in that transition."

## EVALUATING THE AUTHOR'S ARGUMENTS:

**Now that you have read a viewpoint predicting growth of megachurches and a viewpoint predicting growth of home churches, which author do you think is more likely to be correct in his or her predictions? Why?**

# Christianity's Future Will Be Shaped by Non-Western Nations

## Paul Nussbaum

In this viewpoint, Paul Nussbaum presents evidence that the center of power in evangelical Christianity has shifted to non-Western nations, though most Christians in the West are unaware of the shift. The majority of evangelical Christians now live in non-Western countries, he says, where they are transforming Christianity by incorporating local traditions, practices, and beliefs. Non-Western evangelicals also find themselves competing with Islam, raising the possibility of catastrophic conflict. Nussbaum writes for the *Philadelphia Inquirer*.

> *"Most Americans have no idea how big the shift has been."*

**AS YOU READ, CONSIDER THE FOLLOWING QUESTIONS:**

1. How many evangelicals are there in the West compared to the rest of the world, according to the author?
2. In what countries, according to the author, do most evangelicals today live?
3. On what social issues do non-Western evangelicals tend to differ from Western ones?

Evangelical Christianity, born in England and nurtured in the United States, is leaving home.

Most evangelicals now live in China, South Korea, India, Africa and Latin America, where they are transforming their religion. In various ways, they are making evangelical Christianity at once more conservative and more liberal. They are infusing it with local traditions and practices. And they are even sending "reverse missionaries" to Europe and the United States.

## Big Shift

In 1960, there were an estimated 50 million evangelical Christians in the West, and 25 million in the rest of the world; today, there are an estimated 75 million in the West, and 325 million in the rest of the world (representing about 20 percent of the two billion Christians worldwide), according to Robert Kilgore, chairman of the board of the missionary organization Christar.

Other experts differ on the number of evangelicals (estimates range from 250 million to nearly one billion) but agree that the number is growing rapidly.

"As the vibrancy of evangelicalism seems to have waned somewhat in the West, many in the non-West are ready to pick up the banner and move forward," said Kilgore, a former missionary who is now associate provost at Philadelphia Biblical University. "Most Americans have no idea how big the shift has been."

Todd M. Johnson, director of the Center for the Study of Global Christianity, writes that "Africans, Asians and Latin Americans are more typical representatives of evangelicalism than Americans or Europeans."

## Conflicts with Islam

The new evangelicals are more exuberant in their worship services; put more faith in spiritual healing, prophecy and visions; and read the Bible more literally than many of their Western cousins.

And many of the new evangelicals are on the fault lines of global unrest, where cultures and religions collide. Christianity and Islam are often competitors in these developing countries, and some scholars, such as Philip Jenkins of Pennsylvania State University, see the possibility there for cataclysmic conflict.

"A worst-case scenario would include a wave of religious conflicts reminiscent of the Middle Ages, a new age of Christian crusades and Muslim jihads," Jenkins writes in his book, "The Next Christendom: The Coming of Global Christianity." "Imagine the world of the 13th century armed with nuclear warheads and anthrax."

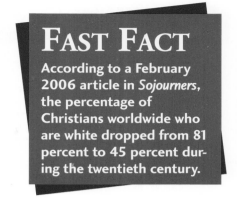

**FAST FACT**

According to a February 2006 article in *Sojourners*, the percentage of Christians worldwide who are white dropped from 81 percent to 45 percent during the twentieth century.

Others think such dire scenarios are far-fetched but see decades of friction ahead as Christianity and Islam compete, especially in Africa and Asia.

## Fastest-Growing Segment

Evangelicals are among the fastest-growing segments of Christianity. Their global numbers are increasing at about 4.7 percent a year, according to Operation World, a Christian statistical compendium.

By comparison, the rate of growth for all Protestants is put at 2.2 percent a year, and for Roman Catholics at 0.5 percent a year. The world's population is growing at about 1.4 percent a year.

Broadly defined, evangelicals are Christians who have had a personal or "born-again" religious conversion, believe that the Bible is the word of God, and believe in spreading their faith. (The term comes from Greek; to "evangelize" means to preach the gospel.) The term is typically applied to Protestants.

## Different Beliefs and Practices

American evangelicals have gotten most of the public attention because they're in the center of the media universe and because they played a pivotal political role in the 2004 U.S. election. But American evangelicals are a distinct minority, and their beliefs and practices are often significantly different from those of evangelicals elsewhere.

In Africa, some evangelicals practice polygamy. In China, some revere their ancestors. In South Korea, many believe in faith healing and the exorcism of evil spirits.

The melding of local traditions with Christianity has produced a

## Expected Changes in Catholic Church Membership During the Next Quarter Century

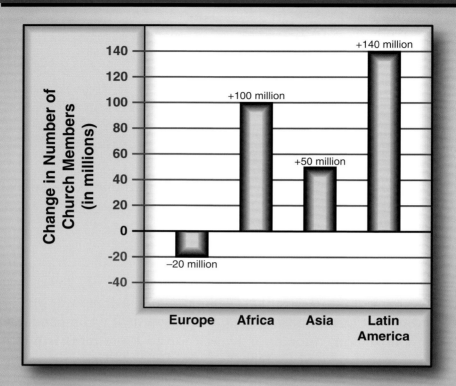

Change in Number of Church Members (in millions)

- 140
- 120
- 100
- 80
- 60
- 40
- 20
- 0
- -20
- -40

+140 million

+100 million

+50 million

−20 million

Europe    Africa    Asia    Latin America

Taken from: Wesley Granberg-Michaelson, Sojourners, February 1, 2006.

religion that looks unfamiliar to many Westerners but is "vast, varied, dynamic and lively," said Joel Carpenter, provost and professor of history at Calvin College, an evangelical college in Grand Rapids, Mich. Carpenter, an editor of "The Changing Face of Christianity," is soon to be director of the new Nagel Institute for the Study of World Christianity at Calvin.

Evangelicals in the global South and East are, in many ways, at least as conservative as their U.S. counterparts. But they often diverge on such issues as poverty and war.

"On abortion or gay marriage, they sound like American conservatives. But on war and peace or economic justice, they sound like the Democratic Party," said Carpenter. "And I have not met one foreign evangelical leader that approves of American foreign policy."

## West Oblivious to Shift

Non-Western evangelicals may already be charting new directions with new leaders that the old bastions of Christianity are unaware of, said Mark Noll, a professor of history at Wheaton College.

"Historically, in unpredictable places and unpredictable times, you get real savvy leaders," Noll said. "I suspect that in Beijing [China], Nairobi [Kenya] or Cape Town [South Africa], things will be very well along with innovation before Philadelphia, Chicago or London is aware of it.

"Almost everything that's significant takes place below the radar screen," he said.

John H. Orme, executive director of the Interdenominational Foreign Mission Association, an alliance of evangelical mission groups, said the old citadels of Christianity could learn from the new.

"I wish the Third World would have more effect on us," he said. "The church in the developing world is much more alive to the working of the holy spirit."

Kilgore said "many Westerners feared they (foreign evangelicals) would mess it up, but the more they've taken their own course, the more it has produced growth. If there is anything that encourages me, it is that Christianity is no longer a U.S. or Canadian or European-dominated religious system."

"We help where we can, but we have to stay away from being Uncle Sam and telling them how to do it."

## Competing with Islam

As the new evangelicals expand their influence and their territory, they face confrontation with other religions, most often Islam. The issue of how the world's two biggest religions will interact "is a fantastically important question," said Lamin Sanneh, the D. Willis James professor of Missions and World Christianity at Yale Divinity School.

Muslims represent about 20 percent of the world's population, compared with Christians' 33 percent. But Islam is growing more rapidly than Christianity, largely because of faster population growth in Muslim countries, and it may surpass Christianity as the world's most popular religion in this century.

Sudan, Nigeria and the Balkans offer recent examples of violence between Christians and Muslims. But there are other examples, such as

*The reality of being a Catholic in Africa can be a hard contrast, given the high rate of HIV infection among the population and the Catholic church's position on contraceptives.*

South Africa, where the two religions coexist peacefully, said Sanneh, a native of Gambia who is the author of *Whose Religion Is Christianity? The Gospel Beyond the West*.

In Islamic countries, the Western notion of separation of church and state is largely unknown, and Sanneh said American Christians ought to better explain the advantages—to both religion and government—of keeping the two separate.

"The American experience on that is relevant to the rest of the world in a remarkable way," Sanneh said. "Americans confronted that centuries before the rest of the world."

## Triumph of the New

After centuries of receiving missionaries from colonial powers in the West, evangelicals in Africa and Latin America and Asia are now planting churches in the United States and Europe. As immigrants arrive here, many bring their own brand of evangelical Christianity with them, while others start churches specifically to minister to "post-Christian" Westerners.

The shift of the global center is unsettling to many American evangelicals used to the old order.

"It will be humbling for the North," said Carpenter.

But he and Noll, the Christian historian at Wheaton, said this latest transformation of evangelical Christianity should be seen less as a loss of the old than a triumph of the new.

"When I'm thinking like a historian, I tend to be a little depressed," Noll said. "But when I'm thinking like a Christian, I tend to be optimistic."

## EVALUATING THE AUTHOR'S ARGUMENTS:

After reading this article, what do you think are the main differences between evangelicals in the West and in non-Western countries? Do you think these differences are helpful or harmful to the future of Christianity? Give reasons for your answers.

Viewpoint

4

# Christianity's Future Will Be Shaped by Women

**Dana L. Robert**

*"Christianity is a women's religion."*

Dana L. Robert argues in this viewpoint that Christianity demographically is a women's religion. Though men often have more leadership roles, women constitute the majority of active participants, she says. The author cites studies showing that women make majorities in Pentecostalism, Catholicism, those who take religious vows, and those who embark on religious pilgrimages. Robert is a professor of World Christianity and History of Mission at Boston University School of Theology.

**AS YOU READ, CONSIDER THE FOLLOWING QUESTIONS:**
1. According to the author, what percentage of practicing Christians are women?
2. To whom has God entrusted the future of humanity according to Bishop Michael Pfeifer, as quoted by the author?
3. According to the author, demographically what nationality and gender is the typical Christian?

Dana L. Robert, "World Christianity as a Women's Movement," *International Bulletin of Missionary Research,* October 1, 2006. Copyright © 2006 Overseas Ministries Study Center. Reproduced by permission.

What would the study of Christianity in Africa, Asia, and Latin America look like if scholars put women into the center of their research? In this article I argue that the current demographic shift in world Christianity should be analyzed as a women's movement, based on the fact that even though men are typically the formal, ordained religious leaders and theologians, women constitute the majority of active participants. First, I examine the evidence for women's presumed majority in world Christianity. Statements that women are "naturally" more religious than men or that women "always" outnumber men in churches need to be analyzed or else they fail to do justice to the complexity and diversity of women's experiences of Christianity. . . .

## Female Majority in Christianity

My statement that the growing world church is largely female was reached by extrapolating from histories of conversion in the nineteenth

*A 2004 census in India showed a marked increase in the number of Christian women.*

and twentieth centuries, with information from regional qualitative studies of rapidly growing groups in Africa and Latin America—in particular, African indigenous churches (AICs) and Latin American Pentecostals. Bengt Sundkler gave the first hint of growing African female participation rates in Bantu Prophets in South Africa (1948), his pioneering study of AICs. Sundkler noted that among Zulus, congregations of historic mission churches were composed mostly of females and were thus referred to by their pastors as "women's church." Female local leaders showed more initiative than men in leading prayer meetings, congregational visitation, and singing. As AICs then broke off from the mission churches, female prophets emerged who believed themselves empowered by the Holy Spirit. David and Bernice Martin, in their groundbreaking empirical studies of the conversion of Latin American Roman Catholics to Pentecostalism, indicated that two-thirds of Pentecostals in Central America were women. Thus I surmised that if the fastest growing indigenous groups in Latin America and Africa were predominantly female, and that if in the year 2000 these continents together contained roughly 41 percent of the world's Christians, then one could speak of the typical Christian in 2000 as a Latin American or African female. Although I used Latin American and African material as sources for my conclusions, the case for a global non-Western female majority was strengthened by other evidence that growing churches in Asia, such as Chinese house churches and Korean cell groups, are also predominantly female. . . .

## Women Majority in Pentecostalism

Studies of Pentecostalism provide strong evidence that there is a female majority in world Christianity today. In his overview, *An Introduction to Pentecostalism: Global Charismatic Christianity*, South African Pentecostal scholar Allan Anderson takes what he calls a "multicultural" rather than a "historical" approach to the subject. . . .

[T]he important point for this article is that [Anderson] unpacks the category of Pentecostal to reveal that three-fourths of them live in the "majority world." Not only are three-quarters of the world's Pentecostals from Africa, Asia, and Latin America, but also "throughout the world, there are many more [Christian] women than [Christian] men." Like so many other studies, the fact of a female majority lies embedded in Anderson's data. He attests that not only is

Pentecostalism the fastest-growing block of Christians in the world, but three-fourths of them live in the "third" world—and of these the vast majority are women.

As he surveys Pentecostalism by region, Anderson occasionally comments on gender ratios. Not only were women the majority of

"apostles" at the Azusa Street revival, but the majority of missionaries who went out as early self-supporting missionaries from Azusa Street were women; Hispanic Pentecostals in North America are predominantly women and children; and Pentecostals in Lagos, Nigeria, are largely women. According to Kwabena Asamoah-Gyadu, who has conducted a major study of indigenous Pentecostalism in Ghana, involvement in Pentecostal and charismatic churches in Ghana runs 60 percent female and 40 percent male . . . .

## Women in Catholicism

In the new appreciation for popular Catholicism, women are . . . hailed as keepers of a flexible cultural continuity for their communities and families. In 1999 Thomas Bamat and Jean-Paul Wiest published a fascinating collection of empirical studies entitled *Popular Catholicism in a World Church*. Seven case studies of Catholic inculturation reveal the high devotion of non-Western Catholics to communal religiosity and to rituals. Unfortunately, even in this fine collection sustained attention to gender is minimal, partly because of a shortage of female researchers for the case studies. The editors of the project do indicate, however, that in popular Catholicism around the world, most participants are women.

Women in popular Catholicism appear to be most active in communal devotions designed to ensure the well-being and health of their families. On the Caribbean island of St. Lucia, for example, women dominate several sodalities. They wear special white uniforms, hold regular novenas to pray for healing and guidance, attend special Masses, and pray for the intervention of the saints. In Tanzania women constitute the majority of the Marian Faith Healing Ministry, a prayer vigil group that asks the Virgin Mary for intervention, prays for healing and exorcism of evil spirits, visits the sick, and testifies. Although the church hierarchy has condemned the Marian group, the women persist in their popular devotions.

## Women Religious Pilgrims

In addition to localized prayer groups and rituals, major Catholic pilgrimage sites document female majorities, especially in relation to prayers for family healing and communal well-being. Lay Catholics in different countries see Mary as a source of both spiritual and emotional strength, and they eagerly participate in pilgrimages, such as Mexican devotion to Our Lady of Guadalupe, Portuguese devotion to Our Lady of Lourdes, and other manifestations of the Virgin Mary. Veneration of Our Lady of Guadalupe, for example, underscores the sacredness of motherhood in Mexican Catholic culture. Records of the annual pilgrimage in Mexico written in 1926 describe thousands of Indian families walking for miles to the shrine in Mexico City, camping out to participate in the 5:00 A.M. Mass. Entering the sanctuary, the pilgrims crawled on their knees toward the shrine, and "numerous women raised their arms aloft in supreme supplication and lifted their faces to heaven while tears streamed down their cheeks." Thomas Tweed's creative study of Our Lady of Charity follows the pilgrimage of the Virgin herself, as devotion to the patron saint of Cuba traveled with exiles to Miami. He notes that in both Cuba and the United States, most pilgrims to the shrine are women, a gender pattern that has existed since the 1800s, when travelers to Cuba noted that women and children filled the churches. Said Bishop Michael Pfeifer of San Antonio in 1994, "God has entrusted the future of humanity to women. Women are the primary evangelizers. . . . Our faith comes primarily from our mothers and grandmothers."

## Women and Religious Vows

One way to reveal the gender breakdown in world Catholicism is to examine the enthusiasm for vowed religious life among non-Western women. Even as the number of nuns is dropping in the West, the number of women in religious orders increased by 56 percent from 1975 to 2000 in Africa, and by 83 percent in Asia. In Africa there are one-third fewer Catholic priests and brothers than there are religious sisters. In Asia priests and brothers number less than three-fifths the number of

## Moms More Spiritual Than Dads

*According to a 2007 survey, mothers are more likely than fathers to:*

- Say they feel greatly transformed by faith

- Say faith is very important in their life

- Be born again

- Say they are absolutely committed to Christianity

- Embrace personal responsibility to share faith in Jesus with others

- Attend church

- Pray

- Read Bible

- Participate in small Church groups

- Attend Sunday school

- Volunteer to help a non-profit organization

Taken from: The Barna Group, Ltd., May 7, 2007.

sisters. Although the gender of religious professionals does not necessarily reflect religious participation among ordinary Catholic laity, the fact that religious sisters far outnumber male religious does indicate the attraction of Catholicism for women. With the overall success of sisters' cross-cultural missions in the twentieth century, many traditionally Western communities of sisters are in the process of becoming non-Western. For example, some congregations of Franciscan sisters are evolving from North American to Brazilian membership. Similar ethnic transitions among female Catholic religious communities are a metaphor for the "Southward shift" in global Catholicism itself.

As with lay pilgrimages, a great attraction to vowed life among non-Western Catholic women lies in their personal identification with the Blessed Virgin Mary, mother of Jesus. Catholic sisters not only look to Mary for spiritual power, but they are themselves also identified as "Marys," as communal rather than biological mothers of their nations. According to an important study of the Sisters of Notre Dame de Namur in the Congo, African sisters are widely seen as "BaMama BaMaseri," or Mamas of all the people. Congolese women's traditional value as "life-bearers" meant that the first African sisters who joined the Belgian order in the 1930s and 1940s were ridiculed as barren women or "sterilized cows." But over time, as local Catholic devotion deepened and the sisters proved themselves as teachers and nurses, they earned the respect of their laity. Congolese sisters see their celibacy not as a loss of "physical maternity" but as "a call to nurture and foster life for all in an unbounded, universal spiritual maternity." According to Ursuline Mother Superior Bernadette Mbuy-Beya of Lubumbashi, the Catholic sister "bears children for the Church" and is thus "at the centre of inculturation in Africa."

## Christianity Is a Women's Religion

Although evidence on gender tends to be anecdotal rather than based on statistical surveys, the overwhelming impression based on a sampling of both regional and ecclesiastical studies is that women constituted roughly a two-thirds majority of practicing Christians in the growing world church in the late twentieth and early twenty-first centuries. From a demographic perspective, Christianity is a women's religion.

## EVALUATING THE AUTHOR'S ARGUMENTS:

After reading this article and the one that preceded it, which do you think will have a greater impact on the future of Christianity—the shift of Christianity to non-Western nations or the growing role of women? Give reasons for your answer.

## Viewpoint

## 5

# The Bible Should Be Taught in School

## Jane Lampman

Jane Lampman argues in this viewpoint that educators believe knowledge of the Bible is essential to understanding Western culture. However, she claims, students have very little knowledge of the Bible and schools are afraid to teach it for fear of violating the people's rights as laid out in the U.S. Constitution. She says teaching the Bible in school is constitutional so long as it is presented objectively as part of secular education, and that schools should add the Bible to their curriculum. Lampman writes for the *Christian Science Monitor*.

*"Without academic knowledge of the Bible and its influence . . . pupils can't under-stand their own literary, artistic, and cultural heritage."*

**AS YOU READ, CONSIDER THE FOLLOWING QUESTIONS:**
1. What percentage of allusions to the Bible appears in one book that helps prepare students to take the Advance Placement Exam, according to the author?

2. How many high schools have adopted elective-course material on the Bible, according to the National Council on Bible Curriculum?
3. What is the name of the Supreme Court case that ruled it was appropriate to teach about the Bible objectively as part of a secular program of education?

Like prayer in the schools and the Ten Commandments in courthouses, teaching about the Bible in public classrooms has long been contentious. Some people question whether it is legal. Many educators worry they might be faced with lawsuits.

And American students, it seems, end up the losers. Without academic knowledge of the Bible and its influence, many teachers say, pupils can't understand their own literary, artistic, and cultural heritage. In a survey last spring, 90 percent of leading English teachers said biblical knowledge was crucial to a good education. Yet a Gallup poll found that only 8 percent of public-school teens said their school offered an elective course on the Bible.

## Making It Constitutional

For school districts, the difficulty lies in agreeing on what will pass constitutional muster, and then actually having the materials to teach it appropriately.

Help may be on the way. The Bible Literacy Project, a nonpartisan, nonprofit group in Fairfax, Va., has spent five years developing the first high school text on the Bible in 30 years. The project involved scholars and reviewers from all major Jewish and Christian traditions.

"The Bible and Its Influence," released . . . [in September 2005] in Washington, is designed to meet constitutional standards and to convey the Scriptures' broad influence on Western civilization. Covering Old and New Testaments, it presents the biblical narratives, characters, and themes as well as their cultural influences.

Students may gain a more nuanced understanding of [the writings of William] Shakespeare, with his 1,300 biblical references; or grasp the import of the Exodus [the post-famine departure of the Israelites out of Egypt] to the African-American experience and musical heritage; or learn how the Bible shaped Abraham Lincoln's vision. They may even recognize a biblical origin for their hometown—Corpus Christi [Texas], New Canaan [Connecticut], and Salem [Oregon], for example.

The new textbook "treats faith perspectives with respect, and . . . informs and instructs, but does not promote religion," says Chuck Stetson, the Project's founder and chairman.

Others express concern: "I don't think the Constitution prohibits the use of this textbook, but I have real doubts about the wisdom of this approach," says Barry Lynn, executive director of Americans United for the Separation of Church and State. "At this time in America, it's better to simply talk about religious influences when they come up during the study of literature, art, and history, and not take the text of one religious tradition and treat it with special deference." Mr. Lynn also worries that individual teachers might go beyond the text itself and "spin it in ways that may well violate the Constitution."

## Students Love It

As part of a pilot effort during textbook development, the Project provided a training program for 27 public high school teachers over an eight-month period. Five of the teachers received a classroom set of the draft text to test with students.

"Students love the material—it's beautiful," says Joan Spence, a language-arts teacher in Battle Ground, Wash. "It is formatted like other textbooks, and puts them in the English-class mindset. They don't have the temptation to wander off into a Sunday School frame of mind."

Ms. Spence taught a Bible literature course for two years before having access to the textbook, and says she appreciates its "wealth of connections to art, poetry, music—the artists who have created out of inspiration from the Bible.

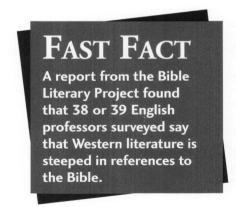

**FAST FACT**

A report from the Bible Literary Project found that 38 or 39 English professors surveyed say that Western literature is steeped in references to the Bible.

## Objectivity Required

More than 40 years ago, the United States Supreme Court said (in *School District of Abingdon*

*Twp. v. Schemp*) that it was appropriate to teach about the Bible as long as it "is presented objectively as part of a secular program of education." Still, some courses given in schools have veered into sectarian territory.

"Some of the courses I've encountered around the country over 20 years would not pass muster in a court of law," says Charles Haynes of Freedom Forum's First Amendment Center. "They're closer to Sunday School than legitimate academic courses."

He sees the new textbook as important "because it's constitutional and educationally sound, and may provide a safe harbor for public schools."

Five years ago, the First Amendment Center—a nonpartisan group that works with schools on religious liberty issues—brought educational and religious groups together to produce a guide, "The Bible

## Parents Give Schools Low Grades on Tough Topics

*Parents of children in public and private schools were asked how well the schools taught tough topics like religion.*

Based on parents of children in public or private school K-12 (N=554).

| | Rating of how well public schools deal with . . . | | | |
|---|---|---|---|---|
| | Evolution | Religion | Sex Education | Homosexuality |
| **Excellent** | 5% | 6% | 7% | 3% |
| **Good** | 26% | 18% | 31% | 14% |
| **Only Fair** | 33% | 24% | 28% | 24% |
| **Poor** | 20% | 39% | 19% | 34% |
| **Don't Know** | 16% | 13% | 15% | 25% |

Taken from: Pew Forum on Religion in Public Life, August 30, 2005.

and Public Schools." The guide provides districts with information and clear standards to help them keep the teaching academic and not devotional. Districts were left to identify their own books or materials.

"I don't think many people feel well prepared to teach a class of this sort," Ms. Spence says, "or have time to research important background information, so this will make more people feel able to take on the challenge."

## Biblical Knowledge Essential

At the same time, many US English teachers express concern that students' deficient biblical knowledge is hampering their education. Marie Wachlin, a professor at Concordia University in Portland, Ore., conducted the national study earlier this year of high school English teachers in which they said biblical knowledge was essential for a good education. Ninety-eight percent also said biblical literacy is a distinct educational advantage.

Biblical allusions permeate Western literature. In a book that prepares students to take the Advanced Placement Exam, 60 percent of the allusions listed are from the Bible. Yet polls in recent years have shown that both students and adult Americans in general have very limited biblical knowledge.

According to many teachers in the national study, if their schools didn't offer courses, "it wasn't from lack of importance or lack of community support, but due to political pressures," Dr. Wachlin says.

Another group now promoting Bible teaching in schools, which is supported by several conservative groups, has stirred controversy. The National Council on Bible Curriculum in Public Schools says its elective-course material has been adopted by some 1,000 high schools. Last month the Texas Freedom Network, a religious-freedom advocacy group, released a report by a professor at Southern Methodist University. The report charges that their material goes beyond academic study to introduce conservative Protestant views, and is not always historically accurate.

In several districts where their materials have been proposed, fights have ensued, according to Dr. Haynes.

"It's not a curriculum, but a long outline of the Bible, and the Bible itself is the textbook," he says. "The secondary sources are mostly

*Bible study in the classroom may lead to stronger friendships in the future.*

from an Evangelical Christian perspective. Schools don't want to be sued—that's the heart of the matter."

## Winning Approval

The Bible Literacy Project's text has won the approval of key leaders from the various strains of Judaism and Christianity, including Evangelicals.

Marc Stern, general counsel of the American Jewish Congress, a constitutional watchdog, says that, "Without question, it can serve as the basis for a constitutional course."

Leland Ryken, professor of English at Wheaton College, an Evangelical school in Illinois, called it an "undisputed triumph of scholarship and presentation."

The question is whether school superintendents and teachers will embrace it. The $50 book, along with a teachers' manual, will be ready for the next school year. A university-based, online teacher-training program will also be available.

## Pioneering Use of the Bible in Classrooms

Tom Wiegman, who has been teaching the "Bible as literature" to high school seniors in Fullerton, Calif., since 1992, has scouted out his own materials. After using the draft of the new book last semester, he intends to get a set for his classroom.

"The students were very positive about it," he says.

To help students make connections between the Bible and their own experience, Mr. Wiegman has them do an allusion project, looking for examples in American culture. They don't have to look far. Last semester one student brought in a video that showed Eve picking the apple from the proverbial tree, on advice of the serpent—from the opening credits to the TV hit, "Desperate Housewives."

### EVALUATING THE AUTHOR'S ARGUMENTS:

The author discusses a textbook that can be used to teach students about the Bible. Is it necessary to have a separate book or class on the Bible to create Bible literacy rather than simply noting allusions to the Bible when they come up in literature, history, or other classes? What are the potential advantages and disadvantages of creating a class specifically on the Bible?

Viewpoint

6

# The Bible Should Not Be Taught in School

**Mark A. Chancey**

*"Courses often end up promoting whatever religious views [the teachers] are most familiar with."*

In this viewpoint, Mark A. Chancey claims that Bible classes in public school frequently advocate sectarian views. Bible classes also often have low academic standards, he says. Chancey argues that decisions regarding which Bible version to teach, what interpretation to present, and representing the Bible as factually accurate promote religious views. In some cases, the author says, the only textbook is the Bible, and teachers without proper academic training rely upon their personal experiences in presenting the material. Chancey teaches at Southern Methodist University.

**AS YOU READ, CONSIDER THE FOLLOWING QUESTIONS:**

1. Out of twenty-five Texas school districts surveyed, according to the author, how many were presenting Bible classes in a non-sectarian manner?
2. How does Judaism fare in most Bible courses, according to the author.

Mark A. Chancey, "Textbook Case," *The Christian Century,* vol. 123, November 14, 2006, pp. 12-13.

3. According to the author, which version of the Bible is used in most courses?

When asked about the Bible course at the local public high school, a West Texas minister told the *Abilene Reporter News*, "My hope is the end result is they read their Bible and start asking questions elsewhere and they become Christians. That's the hope of the community, too."

Sentiments like that would normally not raise an eyebrow. In this case, however, the minister was also the teacher of the course. His comments raise questions about how successful he is in presenting the material "objectively as part of a secular program of education," as required in the 1963 U.S. Supreme Court ruling on the treatment of the Bible in public schools. To what extent is this teacher's presentation of material affected by his hopes that students will adopt his beliefs?

### Bible Classes Are Sectarian

As it turns out, quite a bit. Like almost all of the other public school Bible courses in Texas, this particular course is portrayed by its school district as nonsectarian. The reality is that it is taught primarily from a conservative Protestant perspective. And like most such courses around the country, little has been known about its contents.

To learn what public schools were teaching about the Good Book, Texas Freedom Network [TFN] Education Fund, affiliated with the Austin-based religious liberties advocacy group Texas Freedom Network, surveyed all 1,031 Texas school districts. Districts were asked if they had offered a Bible course in the past five years, and if so to provide information about the course, including the syllabus, tests, handouts, a list of textbooks and videos used and a description of the teacher's qualifications.

## FAST FACT

The First Amendment Center reports that "Bible wars" broke out in the nineteenth century between Protestants and Catholics over whose version of the Bible would be read each morning in American classrooms.

## Should Creationism Be Taught in Schools?

### Favor Teaching Creationism . . .

| | Along with evolution | | Instead of evolution | |
| --- | --- | --- | --- | --- |
| | Favor | Oppose | Favor | Oppose |
| Total | 64% | 26% | 38% | 49% |
| | | | | |
| Among those believing in . . . | | | | |
| Creation | 65% | 26% | 56% | 32% |
| Evolution | 66% | 27% | 22% | 67% |
|    With guidance | 78% | 18% | 35% | 54% |
|    Natural selection | 62% | 33% | 14% | 79% |
| | | | | |
| White Protestant | 67% | 25% | 46% | 43% |
|   Evangelical | 67% | 24% | 60% | 29% |
|   Mainline | 66% | 27% | 26% | 62% |
| White Catholic | 68% | 20% | 31% | 54% |
| Secular | 55% | 30% | 17% | 63% |

Taken from: Pew Forum on Religion and Public Life, August 30, 2005.

Twenty-five districts acknowledged teaching such a course in 2005–2006. TFN sent their materials to me to assess if the courses are being taught in the neutral, nonsectarian manner that, in the words of one court, seeks neither "to disparage or to encourage a commitment to a set of religious beliefs."

Only three of the 25 school districts—Leander, Whiteface and North East (San Antonio)—succeeded in offering nonsectarian courses.

Materials from the other 22 classes revealed serious problems. Many used overtly sectarian curricular materials, such as *Halley's Bible Handbook*, workbooks, or online readings like one titled "Ten Reasons to Believe the Bible," which was assigned in one district. Tests show that the theological claims of such resources were typically presented to students as matters of fact. In some districts the only textbook was the Bible, with the King James and New International versions the most often recommended.

## Whose Bible Is Taught?

Eleven school districts used the curriculum of the National Council on Bible Curriculum in Public Schools [NCBCPS]. A previous examination of this group's course revealed it to be heavily slanted toward fundamentalist Protestant views. . . .

The NCBCPS claims that its course is taught in over 370 school districts across the nation, including 52 in Texas. If that figure for Texas is true, then 41 Texas school officials provided false information to TFN's legally binding open-records request—a very unlikely possibility. The NCBCPS appears to have greatly exaggerated its numbers.

In most courses, the Protestant Bible is assumed to be the standard. Roman Catholic, Eastern Orthodox and Jewish versions of the canon received little if any attention. The Protestant Bible is usually understood from a conservative theological perspective, often that of inerrancy. Two schools, for example, show a video that argues that copyists have made no changes to the biblical text since it was originally inspired by God. Most depict the Bible as straightforward, unproblematic, wholly accurate history. For example, the early version of the NCBCPS curriculum used by one district attempts to persuade students of the plausibility of the story of Noah's ark by asking questions such as "Approximately how many animals were on the ark the size of a rhesus monkey?" Several of the courses are named simply "Bible History."

## Whose Interpretation Is Taught

Dispensationalist premillennialism makes an appearance in a few districts, whether in lectures or Left Behind videos. So does Christian Americanism, the belief that America was founded as a Christian (i.e., conservative Protestant) nation and that its government should return to those roots. Some courses advocate creation science (one lesson plan, for example, focused on the biblical evidence for dinosaurs) and other forms of pseudoscience, such as the claim that the modern races are descended from Noah's sons. At least one school has apparently presented an urban legend as accurate, teaching its students that NASA [National Aeronautics and Space Administration] had discovered a missing day in time that corresponds to the story of the sun standing still in Joshua 10.

Judaism fares particularly poorly in most Bible courses. The Hebrew Bible is almost always read through a Christian lens. The Christian faith claim that the prophets supernaturally predicted the coming of Jesus is presented as fact; Jewish and other interpretations are rarely mentioned. In one district, an essay question instructs students to write about "how God's purpose and plan of the Old Testament has fulfillment in the New Testament." When a test on Genesis includes the question "Write John 3:16," the perspective of the course as a whole is quite clear.

*The separation of church and state is one of the leading reasons given for not teaching religious texts in public schools.*

In several cases, area ministers (almost always Protestants) served as the courses' teachers. More often, the classes were offered by social studies or literature teachers. Only a few had ever had any academic course work in biblical studies.

## Sectarian or Incompetent?

In some courses, the sectarian elements seem intentional, such as the invitation of a creation scientist to be a guest lecturer at one high school and the presentation at another of a lecture titled "God's Road to Life," with the starting point "Jesus Christ is the one and only way." Often, though, problematic elements appear to be the result of a lack of training. The materials sent to TFN suggest that when teachers have no specific academic preparation, they rely primarily upon their personal experiences in shaping and presenting the material. The result is that even when they have the best of intentions, their courses often end up promoting whatever religious views they are the most familiar with.

The religious nature of these courses is not their only problem. Many do not reflect high academic standards. Memorization of Bible verses is usually a major component. Examinations often test retention of details both significant and obscure from Bible stories without encouraging analysis or critical thought. Some courses make questionable use of videos. In a recent school year, students at one school watched videos on one-fifth of the class days. Students at another saw Hanna-Barbera Bible cartoons; those at another viewed Veggie Tales videos, which feature computer-animated talking Christian vegetables.

Texas is not the only state in which Bible courses are taught. A study published by People for the American Way in 2000 discovered 14 Bible courses taught from religious perspectives in Florida. The fact that two studies involving several states and made several years apart had such similar findings suggests that these problems may be widespread elsewhere.

## Support Is Building

In the meantime, public school Bible courses are gaining support from state legislators. In April, Georgia passed a law providing state funding for such courses. Similar bills died in Alabama, Tennessee and Missouri, but are likely to be reintroduced. The Democratic Party of Alabama has already announced a covenant with Alabamans that includes a pledge to increase the number of Bible courses.

Neither the Georgia law nor the other bills explicitly mention funding for teacher training in biblical studies and church-state issues. The assumption seems to be that a teacher's good intentions are sufficient to guarantee that Bible courses will be taught in a nonsectarian and academically sound manner. The lessons from Texas suggest otherwise.

## EVALUATING THE AUTHOR'S ARGUMENTS:

After reading this article and the preceding one, do you think it is possible to teach Bible classes in school without promoting religious views? Why or why not?

# Christian Reconstruction Should Replace Democracy

Gary North

> "Christian Recon- structionists want replacement, not capture, of tax- supported institutions."

Gary North argues in this viewpoint that his five-point biblical covenant theology is the view Christians need to take regarding how representatives should govern. He believes in theocracy, or government by divine guidance or by officials considered divinely guided, not democracy. He contrasts this view with "pre-Christian Right theology," which he says incorrectly teaches democracy and commonsense rationalism. North argues that striking a balance between theocracy and democracy compromises God's law. North is the cofounder of Christian Reconstruction.

## AS YOU READ, CONSIDER THE FOLLOWING QUESTIONS:

1. Under biblical covenant theology, what authority does God give redeemed men?
2. What does the author say is the proper biblical punishment for abortion?
3. According to Christian Reconstructionist Rousas John Rushdoony, as cited by the author, what rival theology is promoted in public schools?

Gary North, "What Went Wrong with the Christian Right," *Faith for All of Life*, January-February 2006. Reproduced by permission.

T he answer is simple: the Christian Right has refused to break with the worst assumptions of the pre-Christian Right.

Before discussing what is wrong, we should discuss what is right. What is right is Biblical covenant theology.

## Biblical Covenant Theology Requires Theocracy

Covenant theology has five points. First, God is absolutely sovereign. That is, He has predestinated everything. He is different from the creation, yet He has entered into the creation, above all through the Second Person of the Trinity's Incarnation as Jesus Christ.

Second, God rules in history covenantally, meaning hierarchically and judicially, primarily through mankind. After the Fall of man, God has dealt with redeemed men in a special way, which includes granting to them the lawful authority to impose judgments in history, including civil judgments.

Third, God has revealed His law for mankind in the Bible, though also in nature. Both man and nature are fallen, which places the Bible, God's Word, as the central source for wisdom and ethics. It alone is trustworthy.

Fourth, as the providential sustainer of the universe, God judicially imputes meaning and then brings salvation (healing, deliverance) to individuals, societies, and nature, based on the comprehensive judgment brought against Jesus Christ at Calvary. We are therefore to think God's thoughts after Him, subordinating our thoughts to the Bible.

Fifth, the new heavens and new earth, announced by Isaiah, will progressively replace Satan's kingdom in history before Jesus comes in final judgment. To put these points in one sentence, the Bible teaches predestination, theocracy, theonomy, presuppositionalism, and post-millennialism.

Covenant theology is an inescapable concept. It is never a question of covenant theology vs. no covenant theology. It is a question of *which* covenant theology.

Having summarized the Bible's doctrine of the covenant, I will now summarize the covenant theology of the pre-Christian Right.

## American Covenant Theology

First, God is not absolutely sovereign. Man's free will acts as a retarding factor on God's decree. God's decree is not comprehensive. God may or may not know the future perfectly, but men are surely sovereign in accepting or rejecting the gospel, and therefore sovereign over less important matters as well.

Second, God rules hierarchically through mankind, but He no longer has selected redeemed men to exercise special authority in civil affairs.

Third, God's revealed law is confined to the Old Testament, which is no longer binding. Mankind is to be ruled by means of natural law, which is common to all men.

Man and nature are fallen, but this has not seriously impaired the operation of natural law, as discovered by fallen man.

Fourth, God imputes meaning to all things and then salvation to individuals, but He does not save societies. Salvation is souls-only. So, in order to maintain society apart from specific redemption, truth must be available to all men on a common-access basis.

Fifth, because God saves souls only, and because the souls saved will remain a minority throughout history, society will remain unredeemed until Jesus comes again.

To put these points in one sentence, the Bible teaches free will, democracy, natural law theory, common-sense rationalism, and pessi-millennialism [the belief that God will save some individuals, but society as a whole will remain unredeemed until Christ returns], pre-millennialism [the belief that Christ will reign as king for a period of time before the world ends], or amillennialism [the belief that the world will end upon Christ's return].

We now turn to the area of applied theology. Each of these rival covenant theologies has undergirded a specific way of looking at the world. Each has produced a rival social outlook: in education, economics, politics, psychology, and popular culture. Each has produced a rival program of reconstruction.

## Christian Reconstruction

Christian Reconstruction (capital R) [a belief in postmillennialism, or that God's kingdom will be established on earth prior to Christ's return] can be said to have appeared as a developed theological system with the publication of Rousas John Rushdoony's book, *The Institutes of Biblical Law* in 1973. That marked the resurrection of a lost Protestant tradition: a 300-year hiatus since the publication of Richard Baxter's *A Christian Directory*, published in 1673. Baxter's book was a work of Protestant casuistry: the application of Christian principles to society.

Rushdoony's first book was on Cornelius Van Til's philosophy: *By What Standard?* (1959). Van Til was a strict presuppositionalist philosopher—unique in church history. He was a true radical. Rushdoony explained and affirmed Van Til's approach: a rejection of natural law theory and all common-ground systems of rationalism. This offered Rushdoony a strategy of reconstruction: education.

His second book—not counting a short extract of *By What Standard?* published as *Van Til* (1960)—was *Intellectual Schizophrenia* (1961), a defense of Christian education and a rejection of public (tax-funded) education. He began with a strategy: replace the public schools. Do not attempt to reform them, he warned. De-fund them. This was a radical position for Christians in 1961. It still is. It is consistent with Van Til's presuppositionalism: no common-ground reasoning.

Rushdoony extended his critique of public education, as no one had before or has since, in *The Messianic Character of American Education* (1963). Here, he showed that humanism has a rival theology, which is redemptive. The public schools serve as an established church for the priesthood of humanist education.

## Establish the Kingdom of God

His strategy of reconstruction for education was simple: "Replacement, not capture." This requires the development of separate Christian schools, programs, and curriculum materials, financed by Christians, not the State. He understood this ancient principle: "He who pays the piper calls the tune." And this one: "If you take the king's shilling, you do the king's bidding."

He maintained this stand with respect to all of his recommended reforms of society's institutions. He did not trust the State to be a positive force. He did not believe in taxation for the purpose of passing out positive sanctions. Again, this had to do with point four of the covenant: evaluation, imputation, and sanctions.

"You can't beat something with nothing." This traditional political maxim applies to every fallen institution. Criticism of evil is not enough. Criticism alone makes you a gravedigger, Rushdoony said on numerous occasions. But Van Til's critique of humanist philosophy was negative. Van Til was like a demolition expert, blowing up the epistemological foundations of humanism's institutions. Rushdoony therefore looked for a way to reconstruct these logically demolished foundations. He turned to ethics: Biblical Law. He began a multi-year series of sermons in 1968, which became *Institutes of Biblical Law*.

Unlike Van Til, an amillennialist, Rushdoony was optimistic that the Kingdom of God will inevitably replace the kingdom of Satan in history. Point five reinforced points four and three, and thereby reinforced the general strategy of Christian Reconstruction: replacement, not capture.

*Many believe that the roots of the United States are in its religious conviction, and believe these religious values should remain in tact in today's society.*

## Other Christians Deny Theocracy

Rushdoony's Calvinism [a belief in God's will] repelled the Arminians [who believe free will plays a role in salvation] in the Creation Science movement. This was true also of the developers of the Christian curriculum movement: Bob Jones University Press, Pensacola Christian School (A Beka), and Accelerated Christian Education. These movements are anti-presuppositional, common-ground movements. Creation Science wants "neutral" facts to convince evolutionists. Fundamentalist educators baptize humanistic conservative ideas, modify their textbooks' content slightly, and present the jumbled mess as "a Christian world and life view."

Finally, there is the issue of theocracy. Point two's hierarchicalism is only partially acceptable to fundamentalist Christians. Oath-bound covenants must be Trinitarian, they insist, to secure individual salvation, family authority, and church authority. But the State must always be neutral with respect to the God of the Bible. Natural law or common-sense rationalism must dominate. Biblical civil law has been annulled.

If common-ground rationalism and common-ground ethics are morally mandatory, then common-ground politics is also mandatory.

This leads us to the Christian Right. . . . .

## The Christian Right Waffles on Abortion

The year 1973 was a crucial year in the development of the Christian Right. In January, the U.S. Supreme Court handed down *Roe v. Wade*, legalizing abortion on demand. Rushdoony had warned that this was coming in the July 1970 issue of the *Chalcedon Report*. No Christian leader paid any attention.

It took several years for Protestant evangelical leaders to become active in the anti-abortion movement. I once heard Tim LaHaye give a speech to a group of pro-life activists in Texas. He admitted that he had for years paid no attention to the ruling.

Abortion brings into the public arena a Van Tilian fact of life: an aborted baby is either dead or alive. There is no neutral ground, no halfway condition, in between dead or alive. The abortion issue was the wedge of Van Tilian self-consciousness for millions of Christians. They gained the first glimmer of awareness regarding a Van Tilian truth applied to civil law: the State is not neutral.

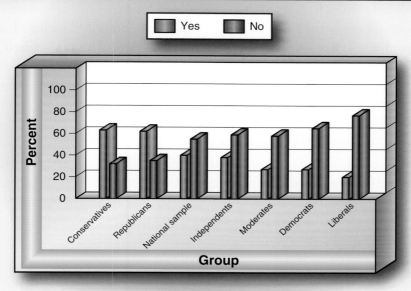

## Should a Political Leader Rely On Religion When Making Policy Decisions?

Yes No

Percent

100
80
60
40
20
0

Conservatives Republicans National sample Independents Moderates Democrats Liberals

**Group**

Taken from: ABC/Washington Post poll, April 2005.

We began to see placards: "Abortion is Murder." But then Christian Reconstructionists (alone) asked that terrifying judicial question: "What Is the proper civil penalty for murder?" The answer was obvious: execution. The anti-abortionist leaders all began to waffle, and they have waffled ever since.

The pro-life movement has become almost invisible today, a pale reflection of what it was in 1985. Its leaders refuse to deal with the obvious judicial implication of those early placards, which we rarely see today.

## Biblical Law, Not Supreme Court Law

In a world governed by a 5–4 vote of the U.S. Supreme Court, pro-life activists seek deliverance by a constitutional amendment. But this is not going to happen, and the leaders know it. "Thus saith the Court" has more authority today than "Thus saith the Lord." The pro-life leaders refuse to go to Exodus 21, the only passage in the Bible that clearly provides a judicial answer to abortion, the passage that Rushdoony cited in 1970.

If men strive, and hurt a woman with child, so that her fruit depart from her, and yet no mischief follow: he shall be surely punished, according as the woman's husband will lay upon him; and he shall pay as the judges determine. And if any mischief follow, then thou shalt give life for life, eye for eye, tooth for tooth, hand for hand, foot for foot, burning for burning, wound for wound, stripe for stripe. (Exodus 21:22-25).

"Eye for eye? Why, that's Old Testament stuff!" Indeed it is. And so the pro-life movement has become just one more special-interest political fundraising group. Its leaders refuse to offer Biblical support for their proposed constitutional reconstruction. Why? Because if you cite Exodus 21 as morally binding on America, you are stuck with Exodus 22.

Thou shalt not suffer a witch to live. (Exodus 22:18)

Whosoever lieth with a beast shall surely be put to death. (Exodus 22:19)

He that sacrificeth unto any god, save unto the LORD only, he shall be utterly destroyed. (Exodus 22:20)

## Democracy Compromises God's Law

The pro-life leaders are not about to get pulled into Exodus 22. So, they send out fundraising letters and propose strategies that have failed before and will fail again. They propose more of the same. But the longer this holocaust goes on, the larger the number of Christians who have nieces and granddaughters who have had an abortion. The oldsters therefore begin to accept abortion "in special circumstances," which all boil down to this one: "Pregnancy of someone related to me."

Leader by leader, issue by issue, the Christian Right turns to political alliances with humanists in the Republican Party. They are now facing the situation that Blacks face in the Democratic Party: "When you are in a political Party's hip pocket, you will be sat on."

The Christian Right wants a halfway house between democracy and theocracy. It also wants a halfway house between theonomy and autonomy, revelation and rationalism, creationism and evolutionism. It wants equal time for Jesus, which means equal time for Satan.

Their allies, the humanists, want no time for Jesus. They want the votes and donations of the faithful, but nothing more. They generally get what they want. . . .

We see the outworking of two rival Christian covenants: two rival strategies. The Christian Reconstructionists want replacement, not capture, of tax-supported institutions. The Christian Right wants capture, but with shared power as the price.

## EVALUATING THE AUTHOR'S ARGUMENTS:

The author claims that the Bible is the only trustworthy source for wisdom and ethics. He also contrasts biblical covenant theology with what he calls the covenant theology of the pre-Christian right. Are these two views both based on the Bible? Do you believe the author proves why his view is correct and the other is not?

# Christian Reconstruction Threatens Freedom

**John Sugg**

> *"We [will] train up a generation . . . which finally denies the religious liberty of the enemies of God."*

In this viewpoint John Sugg argues that Christian Reconstructionists seek to replace democracy with theocracy, in which God's law, as they interpret it, will be the government's law. Sugg says Reconstructionists oppose freedom of expression and support state religious creeds. Reconstructionists and their sympathizers dominate the Republican Party in many states, he says. According to the author, Reconstructionists call for nothing less than overthrow of the United States of America. Sugg is a Group Senior Editor of CL Newspapers/CL Media.

## AS YOU READ, CONSIDER THE FOLLOWING QUESTIONS:

1. What did Reconstructionist Rousas J. Rushdoony call democracy, according to the author?
2. What do Reconstructionists think should be done with non-believers and homosexuals?

John Sugg, "Warped Worldview: Christian Reconstructionists Believe Democracy is Heresy, Public Schools are Satanic and Stoning Isn't Just for the Taliban Anymore—and They've Got More Influence Than You Think," *Church & State,* vol. 59, July 1, 2006, pp. 11-13. Copyright 2006 Americans United for Separation of Church and State. Reproduced by permission.

3. With what Islamic militant group does the author compare Reconstructionists?

Two really devilish guys materialized in Toccoa, Ga., last month to harangue 600 true believers on the gospel of a thoroughly theocratic America. Along with lesser lights of the religious far right who spoke at American Vision's "Worldview Super Conference 2006," Herb Titus and Gary North called for nothing short of the overthrow of the United States of America.

## Replacing the System

Titus and North aren't household names. But Titus, former dean of TV preacher Pat Robertson's Regent University law school, has led the legal battle to plant the Ten Commandants in county courthouses across the nation. North, an apostle of the creed called Christian Reconstructionism, is one of the most influential elders of American fundamentalism.

"I don't want to capture their (mainstream Americans') system. I want to replace it," fumed North to a cheering audience. North has called for the stoning of gays and nonbelievers (rocks are cheap and plentiful, he has observed). Both friends and foes label him "Scary Gary."

Are we in danger of an American Taliban*? Probably not today. But Alabama's "Ten Commandments Judge" Roy Moore is aligned with this congregation, and one-third of Alabama Republicans who voted in the June primary supported him. When you see the South Dakota legislature outlaw abortions, the Reconstructionist agenda is at work. The movement's greatest success is in Christian home schooling, where many, if not most, of the textbooks are Reconstructionist-authored tomes.

## Democracy is Heresy

Moreover, the Reconstructionists are the folks behind attacks on science and public education. They're allied with proselytizers who have tried to convert Air Force cadets—future pilots with fingers on nuclear triggers—into religious zealots. Like the communists of the 1930s, they exert

*an Islamic militant group in Afghanistan

## Have Christians Gone Too Far?

*When asked if conservative Christians have gone too far in trying to impose their religious values on the country, survey respondents said:*

|  | Yes % | No % | Don't Know % |
|---|---|---|---|
| Total | 45 | 45 | 10 |
| White | 43 | 47 | 10 |
| Black | 48 | 40 | 12 |
| College grad | 60 | 35 | 5 |
| Some college | 48 | 45 | 7 |
| H.S. or less | 35 | 50 | 15 |
| Northwest | 48 | 38 | 14 |
| Midwest | 41 | 47 | 12 |
| South | 39 | 52 | 9 |
| West | 55 | 35 | 10 |
| Republican | 26 | 65 | 9 |
|    Conservative | 16 | 76 | 8 |
|    Mod/Liberal | 47 | 43 | 10 |
| Democrat | 57 | 35 | 8 |
|    Mod/Conserv | 46 | 44 | 10 |
|    Liberal | 83 | 16 | 1 |
| Independent | 55 | 35 | 10 |
| White Protestant | 33 | 58 | 9 |
|    Evangelical | 21 | 70 | 9 |
|    Mainline | 50 | 41 | 9 |
| White Catholic | 47 | 42 | 11 |
| Secular | 61 | 27 | 12 |

Taken from: Pew Forum on Religion and Public Life, August 30, 2005.

tremendous stealth political gravity, drawing many sympathizers in their wake, and their friends now dominate the Republican Party in many states.

Titus' and North's speeches, laced with conspiracy theories about the Rockefellers and the Trilateral Commission, were more Leninist than Christian in the tactics proposed—as in their vision to use freedom to destroy the freedom of others. That's not surprising—the founder of Christian Reconstruction, the late fringe Calvinist theologian Rousas J. Rushdoony, railed against the "heresy" of democracy.

A Harvard-bred lawyer whose most famous client is Alabama's Judge Moore, Titus told the Toccoa gathering that the Second Amendment envisions the assassination of "tyrants;" that's why we have guns. Tyranny, of course, is subjective to these folks. Their imposition of a theocratic state would not, by their standards, be tyranny. Public schools, on the other hand, to them are tyrannical. . . .

## Bible Permits Slavery

Hosting the "Creation to Revelation . . . Connecting the Dots" event was a Powder Springs, Ga., publishing house, American Vision, whose pontiff is Gary DeMar. The outfit touts the antebellum South as a righteous society and favors the reintroduction of some forms of slavery (it's sanctioned in the Bible, Reconstructionists say)—which may explain the blindingly monochrome audience at the gathering.

The setting was the Georgia Baptist Conference Center, a sprawling expanse of woods, hills and a man-made lake in the North Georgia mountains. Four decades ago, the Southern Baptists officially declared, "no ecclesiastical group or denomination should be favored by the state" and "the church should not resort to the civil power to carry on its work."

Times change. The Baptists lust for power, and they demand the state to do their bidding. I guess that explains the denomination's hosting of theocrats no less rigid and bloodthirsty than the Taliban's mullahs.

## Clash of Worldviews and Conspiracies

DeMar christened the gathering with invective against science.

"Evolution is as religious as Christianity," he said, a claim that certainly must amaze 99.99 percent of the scientific community. Science is irrelevant to these folks. Everything they need to know about the universe and the origin of man is in the first two chapters of Genesis. They know the answer before any question is asked.

DeMar's spin is what he calls a clash of "worldviews." According to DeMar and his speakers, God sanctions only their worldview. And that worldview is a hash of enforcing Old Testament Mosaic law (except when it comes to chowing down on pork barbecue), rewriting American history to endorse theocracy and explaining politics by the loopy theories of the John Birch Society*. . . .

At the heart of what was taught by a succession of speakers:

- Six-day, "young earth" creationism is the only acceptable doctrine for Christians. Even "intelligent design" or "old earth" creationism are compromises with evil secularism.
- Public education is satanic and must be destroyed.
- The First Amendment was intended to keep the federal government from imposing a national religion, but states should be free to foster a religious creed. (Several states did that during the colonial period and the nation's early days, a model the Reconstructionists want to emulate.)
- The Founding Fathers intended to protect only the liberties of the established ultra-conservative denominations of that time. Expanding the list to include "liberal" Protestant denominations, much less Catholics, Jews and (gasp!) atheists, is a corruption of the Founders' intent.

Education earned the most vitriol at the conference. Effusing that the Religious Right has captured politics and much of the media, North proclaimed: "The only thing they (secularists) have still got a grip on is the university system." Academic doctorates, he contended, are a conspiracy fomented by the Rockefeller family. All academic programs (except, he said, engineering) are now dominated by secularists and Darwinists.

---

*a conservative anti-communism organization

*The freedom to believe as one sees fit (within legal constraint) is the right of every American.*

"Marxists in the English departments!" he ranted. "Close every public school in America!"

## Replace Freedom with God

Among North's most quoted writings was this ditty from 1982: "[W]e must use the doctrine of religious liberty to gain independence for Christian schools until we train up a generation . . . which finally denies the religious liberty of the enemies of God."

Titus followed that party line when he proclaimed that the First Amendment is limited to guaranteeing "the right to criticize the government," but "free expression is not in the Constitution." When I asked him if blasphemy—castigating religion—was protected, he shook his head.

Like North, Titus sees public education as decidedly satanic. Also, welfare. He contended the Founding Fathers—and Americans today—

owe their "first duties to God. It's not just worship. It's education . . . welfare to the poor. Welfare belongs exclusively to God. Why do schools fail? They're trying to do the business of God. Medicaid goes. Education goes. The church gets back to doing what it should do."

And what should the church be doing? According to these self-appointed arbiters of God's will, running our lives. And stoning those who disagree. . . .

**EVALUATING THE AUTHOR'S ARGUMENTS:**

After reading this viewpoint and the preceding one, do you think democracy should be replaced with a theocracy? Are the views of the two authors reconcilable? Why or why not?

# Facts About Christianity

## Facts About the Bible:

According to a survey by Barna Research:

- 71 percent of those who attended high school or less believe the Bible is totally accurate in all of its teachings; only 52 percent of those who have graduated from college believe this.
- 82 percent of African Americans—compared with 68 percent of whites, 62 percent of Hispanics, and 39 percent of Asian Americans—believe the Bible is totally accurate in all of its teachings.
- 78 percent of Republicans and 69 percent of Democrats believe in the Bible's accuracy.
- 96 percent of evangelicals reported reading the Bible during the past week.
- 51 percent of women and 42 percent of men reported reading the Bible during the past week.
- 35 percent of persons who adhere to a non-Christian faith reported reading the Bible during the past week.
- 66 percent of African Americans, 45 percent of whites, 41 percent of Hispanics and 20 percent of Asian Americans reported reading the Bible during the past week.
- 62 percent of Protestants and 28 percent of Catholics reported reading the Bible during the past week.

## Facts About Beliefs:

According to surveys by Barna Research:

- 10 percent of the adults nationwide are atheist or agnostic.
- 10 percent of the U.S. population adheres to a faith other than Christianity.
- When asked whether a person who is generally good or does enough good things for others during his or her lifetime will earn a place in heaven, 54 percent agreed and 40 percent disagreed.
- 55 percent of all adults believe they have a personal responsibility to tell other people about their religious beliefs, with Republicans

being more likely than Democrats to have such a view; 57 percent of African Americans, 37 percent of Hispanics, 36 percent of whites, and 23 percent of Asian Americans feel strongly that they have a personal responsibility to share their religious beliefs with others.

- 71 percent of Americans believe God is the all-powerful, all-knowing, perfect creator that rules the world; 8 percent believe that God is an attainable higher state of consciousness; 7 percent believe that God is the total realization of a person's human potential; 4 percent believe that there is no such thing as God; 4 percent believe everyone is God; and 2 percent believe that there are many gods, each with different power and authority.
- 41 percent of adults believe that Jesus Christ committed sins, with 43 percent of Hispanics, 43 percent of whites, and 32 percent of African Americans holding such a belief.
- 55 percent of adults say that the devil, or Satan, is not a living being but only a symbol of evil; 45 percent of born-again Christians deny Satan's existence and 68 percent of Catholics say the devil is non-existent and only a symbol of evil.

### Facts About Church Attendance

According to a Gallup poll:
- 42 percent of Americans say they attend church or synagogue once a week or almost every week; 43 percent say they seldom or never attend worship services.
- 58 percent of Americans in Alabama, Louisiana, and South Carolina say they attend church weekly or almost weekly; 57 percent of those in Mississippi say the same; 55 percent of those in Utah—a predominantly Mormon state—say they attend weekly or almost weekly.
- Only 24 percent of Americans in New Hampshire and Vermont say they attend worship services weekly or almost weekly; 27 percent in Nevada and 28 percent in Rhode Island say the same.

Surveys by Barna Research report:
- 62 percent of Republicans and 47 percent of Democrats attended church during a typical weekend.
- Catholics and Protestants had the same likelihood of attending church during 2006.
- By region, 54 percent of those in the Midwest, 51 percent of those

in the South, 41 percent of those in the Northeast, and 39 percent of those in the West are likely to attend church during a typical weekend.

## Facts About Different Denominations of Christianity:

According to the Center for the Study of Global Christianity:
- Three countries have more than 200 denominations of Christianity: The United States (635); India (263); and Great Britain (235).
- Countries with between 100 and 200 denominations of Christianity are Japan (179); South Africa (178); the Philippines (176); Canada (145); Nigeria (145); China (141); Brazil (130); France (130); Kenya (128); Indonesia (119); Australia (109); Ghana (109); South Korea (109); and Chile (108).

## Facts About Catholic Priests

According to Georgetown University's Center for Applied Research in the Apostolate:
- The total of all Catholic priests worldwide declined from 270,924 in 1970 to 265,782 in 2000; during the same period, the population of Catholics worldwide increased from 653 million to 1.045 billion; the number of parishes without resident priests worldwide increased from 94,846 to 105, 530.
- The total of all Catholic priests in the United States declined from 35,925 in 1965 to 29,285 in 2003; during the same period, the number of Catholics in the United States increased from 45.6 million to 63.4 million.
- The number of priestly ordinations in the United States declined from 994 in 1965 to 441 in 2003; the number of U.S. parishes without a resident priest increased during the same period front 549 to 3,040.

# Glossary

**celibacy:** abstention from sexual intercourse or abstention by vow from marriage.

**democracy:** a government in which power is invested in the people and exercised by them directly or indirectly through freely elected representatives.

**doctrine:** a principle or position, or a body of principles and positions, in a system of belief or knowledge.

**dogma:** a doctrine or body of doctrines concerning faith or morals formally stated and authoritatively proclaimed by a church.

**evangelical:** characterized by an emphasis on salvation by faith in the atoning death of Jesus Christ through personal conviction, inerrant biblical authority, and the duty to give testimony of their faith to others.

**gay marriage:** marriage between two people of the same sex.

**homosexuality:** the tendency to direct sexual desire toward another person of the same sex.

**megachurch:** any church having an average weekly attendance of two thousand or more congregants.

**ordain:** to invest officially with ministerial or priestly authority.

**prosperity theology:** the doctrine that God intends people to enjoy prosperity, material wealth, and financial success.

**salvation:** deliverance from the power and effects of sin.

**scripture:** the books of the Bible.

**sect:** a group adhering to a distinctive doctrine or to a leader.

**secular:** related to worldly or temporal concerns.

**separation of church and state:** the doctrine that religious and governmental institutions should be kept separate and independent from one another.

# Organizations to Contact

**Americans United for Separation of Church and State**
518 C St. NE, Washington, DC 20002
(202) 466-3234 • fax: (202) 466-2587
e-mail: americansunited@au.org • Web site: www.au.org
This organization promotes the separation of church and state by working on a wide range of pressing political and social issues. The group provides articles, brochures, and other resources on topics such as school prayer, faith-based initiatives, religion in public education, and evolution versus intelligent design.

**Campus Crusade for Christ**
100 Lake Hart Dr., Orlando, FL 32832
(888) 278-7233
Web site: www.ccci.org
Campus Crusade for Christ is an interdenominational group with a network of campus ministries on more than one thousand campuses in the United States and abroad. It includes specialized ministries such as Athletes in Action and provides training for worldwide mission work.

**The Center for Progressive Christianity**
TCPC Office
4916 Pt. Fosdick Dr. NW, Suite 148, Gig Harbor, WA 98335
(253) 303-0022
Web site: www.tcpc.org
The center provides guiding ideas, networking opportunities, and resources for progressive churches, organizations, individuals, and others with a connection to Christianity. The organization has regional and local groups and affiliates. Resources include articles and books for purchase on topics including spiritual exploration and practice, theology, organizational leadership and development, and social and environmental ministry.

## Christian Alliance for Progress

PO Box 40495, Jacksonville, FL 32203-0495

(888) 301-0108

e-mail: infor@christianalliance.org • Web site: www.christianalliance
.org

This group promotes a progressive view of the Gospel. Among issues addressed on its Web site are economic justice, environmental stewardship, and equality for gays and lesbians. Resources include articles on issues of interest to progressive Christians and opportunities to take action on specific issues.

## Christian Coalition of America

PO Box 37030, Washington D.C. 20013-7030

(202) 479-6900 • fax: (202) 479-4260

e-mail: Coalition@cc.org • Web site: www.cc.org

The organization is one of the largest and most active conservative grassroots political organizations in America. The site has news, articles, and information about issues of interest to conservative Christians. It also provides information on how Christians can become involved in the political process, join local Christian Coalition chapters, and contact legislators regarding legislation of interest to conservative Christians.

## Church Women United

The Interchurch Center

475 Riverside Dr., Suite 1626A, New York, NY 10115

(800) 298-5551 • fax: (212) 870-2338

e-mail: cwu@churchwomen.org • Web site: www.churchwomen.org

Church Women United is a racially, culturally, and theologically inclusive biblically-based Christian women's movement, celebrating unity in diversity and working for a world of peace and justice. The group has more than twelve hundred state and local units working for peace and justice in the United States and Puerto Rico.

## Evangelicals for Social Action (ESA)

The Sider Center on Ministry and Public Policy

6 E. Lancaster Ave., Wynnewood, PA 19096-3420

(610) 645-9390 • fax: (610) 649-8090

e-mail: esa@esa-online.org • Web site: www.esa-online.org
Evangelicals for Social Action is an association of Christians seeking to promote Christian engagement, analysis and understanding of major social, cultural, and public policy issues. ESA's board of directors includes many prominent leaders of moderate and progressive evangelicalism. The group emphasizes both the transformation of human lives through personal faith and also the importance of a commitment to social and economic justice as an outgrowth of Christian faith.

## Family Research Council (FRC)
801 G St. NW, Washington, DC. 20001
(202) 393-2100 • fax: (202) 393-2134
Web site: www.frc.org
The Family Research Council promotes public debate and formulates public policy that upholds the institutions of marriage and the family. FRC also promotes the Judeo-Christian worldview as the basis for a just, free, and stable society. Articles and publications relevant to these issues are provided by FRC and available on its Web site.

## Fellowship of Christian Athletes (FCA)
FCA World Headquarters
8701 Leeds Rd., Kansas City, MO 64129
(800) 289–0909 • fax: (816) 921-8755
e-mail: fca@fca.org • Web site: www.fca.org
The Fellowship of Christian Athletes helps coaches and athletes on the professional, college, high school, junior high, and youth levels to use the medium of athletics to promote Christianity. FCA is the largest Christian sports organization in America, with local chapters nationwide

## Focus on the Family
Colorado Springs, CO 80995
(800) 232-6459
Web site:www.family.org
Focus on the Family, founded by Dr. James Dobson, provides articles, resources, and help regarding parenting, relationships and marriage, life challenges, faith, entertainment, and social issues. Resources include magazines, books, CDs and DVDs, and radio and TV broadcasts.

## FutureChurch

17307 Madison Ave., Lakewood OH 44107
(216) 228-0869 • fax: (216) 228-4872
e-mail: info@futurechurch.org • Web site: www.futurechurch.org
FutureChurch is an organization focusing on women in the ministry, optional celibacy, the priest shortage, inclusive language, and Church decision making that involves all believers. Its Web site has articles, news, surveys, and other information on these issues that can be accessed by article or through a keyword search.

## The Interfaith Alliance & The Interfaith Alliance Foundation

1331 H St. NW, 1lth Fl., Washington, DC 20005
(800) 510-0969 • fax: (202) 639-6375
e-mail: info@interfaithalliance.org • Web site: www.interfaithalliance
.org
The Interfaith Alliance, a nondenominational group with members representing more that seventy-five different religions and belief systems, promotes the positive and healing role of religion in public life by encouraging civic participation, facilitating community activism, and challenging religious political extremism.

## The Moral Majority Coalition

1971 University Blvd., Lynchburg VA 24502
Web site: www.moralmajority.us
Moral Majority is dedicated to recruiting and mobilizing social conservatives to promote pro-family, pro-life, strong national defense, and pro-Israel policies. The group promotes voter registration, "get out the vote" campaigns, and prayer for the moral welfare of the nation. Resources include a monthly newspaper called the *National Liberty Journal*.

## Sojourners

3333 14th St. NW, Suite 200, Washington DC 20010
(800) 714-7474 • fax: (202) 328-8757
e-mail: sojourners@sojo.net • Web site: www.sojo.net
Sojourners supports the biblical call to social justice, promoting hope, and building a movement to transform individuals, communities, the

church, and the world. It publishes *Sojourners* magazine and provides other resources addressing the issues of faith, politics and culture from a biblical prospective.

**Women Priests**
HOUSETOP
111A. High St., Rickmansworth
HERTS WD3 1AN, UK
(0044) 1923-779446
Web site: www.womenpriests.org
Women Priests is an international organization promoting ordination of women as priests in the Catholic Church. Its Web site offers articles and books about the ordination of women as well as resources that can be used to advocate the ordination of women.

# For Further Reading

## Books

Brooke Allen, *Moral Minority: Our Skeptical Founding Fathers*, Chicago, Ivan R. Dee, 2006. Presents historical evidence regarding the religious views of the Founding Fathers.

Dana Butler Bass, *Christianity, for the Rest of Us: How the Neighborhood Church Is Transforming the Faith*, San Francisco: HarperCollins, 2006. Presents evidence that the small mainline Protestant neighborhood church is thriving, notwithstanding the reported trends towards mega-churches.

Angela Bonavoglia, *Good Catholic Girls*. New York: HarperCollins 2005. Describes the activities of women fighting to change the role of women in the Catholic Church.

Lew Daly, *God and the Welfare State*. Cambridge: Massachusetts Institute of Technology, 2006. Describes the historical basis of faith-based initiatives.

Newt Gingrich, *Rediscovering God in America*. Nashville, TN: Integrity House, 2006. Argues that America was decisively shaped by the Founding Fathers' belief that the United States is a nation under God.

Michelle Goldberg, *Kingdom Coming: The Rise of Christian Nationalism*. New York: W.W. Norton, 2006 The author chronicles the rise of Christian Nationalism and details the ways in which it is supported by Republican political patronage.

Darryl Hart, *A Secular Faith: Why Christianity Favors the Separation of Church and State*. Chicago: Ivan R. Dee, 2006. The author presents a faith-based argument for keeping Christianity out of politics.

Phillip Jenkins, *The Next Christendom: The Coming of Global Christianity*. New York: Oxford University Press, 2000. The author describes how the future of Christianity will be shaped by the Southern Hemisphere, especially in the Philippines, sub-Saharan Africa, and Latin America.

David G. Myers and Letha Dawson Scanzoni, *What God Has Joined*

*Together? A Christian Case for Gay Marriage.* San Francisco, HarperCollins, 2006. Argues that gay marriage is consistent with Christianity and psychological health.

James M. Robinson, *The Gospel of Jesus: In Search of the Original Good News.* San Francisco: HarperCollins, 2006. The author, a scholar on the earliest sources of information about Jesus, draws upon a combination of ancient and authentic texts to explain his opinion of what Jesus proclaimed and what he might say were he here today.

Ray Suarez, *Holy Vote: The Politics of Faith in America.* New York: HarperCollins, 2006. Examines how the collision between organized religion and politics is transforming America.

Kathleen Kennedy Townsend, *Failing America's Faithful: How Today's Churches Are Mixing God with Politics and Losing Their Way.* New York: Warner, 2007. Author criticizes churches that focus on legal and legislative battles over narrow issues while ignoring social and economic justice and service to others.

## Periodicals

Alexander Alter, "Hispanics Changing Face of Christianity: U.S. Hispanics Are Seeking More Charismatic Worship Services in Congregations That Reflect Their Ethnic Heritage," *Miami Herald*, April 26, 2007.

Nate Anderson, "Meet the Patriot Pastors," *Christianity Today*, November 2006.

Paul Asay, "Home-Church Movement Growing in America," *(Colorado Springs, CO) Gazette,* April 11, 2007.

Dana Blanton, "Courts Driving Religion Out of Public Life; Christianity Under Attack," www.foxnews.com, October 1, 2005.

Rob Boston, "Is the Religious Right Dead? Hardly, Say Church-State Experts as GOP Presidential Candidates Pray for the Fundamentalist Movement's Blessing," *Church and State*, April 2007.

Alan Carlson, "The End of Marriage," *Touchstone: A Journal of Mere Christianity*, September 2006.

Gordon Copeland, "Jesus and Politics," *Stimulus: The New Zealand Journal of Christian Thought and Practice*, August 2006.

*Dallas Morning News,* "Christianity's Growth Has Political Implications," March 6, 2007.

Jim Duffy, "Concept of Same-Sex Marriage Has a Long History," *Irish Times*, December 13, 2006.

Nancy Gibbs, "The Religion Test," *Time*, May 21, 2007.

Dan Gilgoff, "The Preacher Who Put God in Politics," *U.S. News and World Report*, May 28, 2007.

Kathy Lynn Grossman, "God and Gays Churchgoers Stand Divided," *USA Today*, June 13, 2006.

Mark Guydish, "Why? Because the Church Says So That's Why," *(Wilkes-Barre, PA) Times-Leader*, August 7, 2006.

Charles C. Haynes, "Georgia's Bible Bill, *Human Rights: Journal of Section of Individual Rights & Responsibilities*, Summer 2006.

Tom Heinen, "Trading Pews for Couches: More Faithful Are Gathering for Home-Based Worship," *The Milwaukee Journal Sentinel*, April 8, 2007.

Collette M. Jenkins, "More Women Finding Paths into Ministry: Although Denominations Report Increase in Female Clergy, Not All Open to Much-Debated Idea," *Akron (Ohio) Beacon Journal*, June 28, 2006

Franz Klein, "Celibacy & the Future of the Priesthood: John Paul II Priests," *Commonweal*, August 12, 2005.

Charlie Lee-Potter, "It's a Woman's Job Now," *New Statesman, June 26, 2006.*

Rebecca Rosen Lum, "Women Priests Challenge Tradition," *Contra Costa (CA) Times*, August 29, 2006.

William McKenzie, "Religious Thinkers Have a Role for 2008: Like Niebuhr, Theologians Can Help Clarify Politics," *Dallas Morning News*, February 20, 2007.

Gary Mills, "Choosing Sides," *Touchstone: A Journal of Mere Christianity*, March 2007.

Richard John Neuhaus, "Christ Without Culture," *First Things: A Monthly Journal of Religion and Public Life*, April 2007.

Gary North, "What Went Wrong with the Christian Right, *Chalcedon Foundation*, January/February 2006.

Joe Pisani, "A Fair Examination of the Priest Celibacy Issue," *(Stamford, CT) Advocate*, September 29, 2006.

Sarah Posner, "The Religious Right Goes to Washington," *Humanist*, November/December 2006.

Luiz Sergio Solimeo, "Tracing the Glorious Origins of Celibacy," American Society for the Defense of Traditional Family and Property, www.tfp.org 2007.

Gila Stopler, "The Liberal Bind: The Conflict Between Women's Rights and Patriarchal Religion in the Liberal State," *Social Theory and Practice*, April 1, 2005.

John Sugg, "Warped Worldview: Christian Reconstructionists Believe Democracy Is Heresy, Public Schools Are Satanic and Stoning Isn't Just for the Taliban Anymore and They've Got More Influence than You Think," *Church & State*, July 1, 2006.

Cal Thomas, "Church, State, and the Legacy of Jerry Falwell," *USA Today*, May 16, 2007.

Yusufu Taraki, "African Christianity in Global Religious and Cultural Conflict," *Evangelical Review of Theology*, April 2007.

Kim Vo, "Evangelical Trend by Latinos Could Impact Politics: Study Says Growing Numbers Prefer Charismatic Worship," *San Jose Mercury News*, April 26, 2007.

George Weigel, "A Jesus Beyond Politics," *Newsweek*, May 21, 2007.

Jacob Weisberg, "Evolution vs. Religion: Quit Pretending They're Compatible," *Slate,* August 10, 2005.

## Web Sites

**Adherents.com** (http://www.adherents.com/). This site has a collection of statistics on religious affiliation worldwide, searchable by religion and by geographic location.

**Association of Religious Data Archives** (http://www.thearda.com/index.asp). This site provides a great deal of statistics and survey results concerning Christianity.

**Beliefnet.com** (www.beliefnet.com). Beliefnet is a large spiritual Web site not affiliated with any religion or spiritual organization that provides information, articles, and commentary about all religions. The database's search engine can be used to find articles on faith in politics, celibacy, women in the church, trends in Christianity, and other topics.

**Christianity Today** (www.christianitytoday.com). This site of the magazine *Christianity Today* has articles, news, and opinions about issues in Christianity.

**Religioustolerance.org** (http://www.religioustolerance.org). The site has over three thousand essays and articles on religions, religious beliefs, and issues of interest to religious groups, such as abortion, the death penalty, and same-sex marriage.

**World Christian Database** (http://www.worldchristiandatabase.org). World Christian Database provides comprehensive statistical information on world religions, Christian denominations, and people groups.

# Index

# Picture Credits

Cover: Reproduced by permission of photos.com
All photos © AP Images